Making Learning Stick

20 Easy and Effective Techniques for Training Transfer

Making Learning Stick

20 Easy and Effective Techniques for Training Transfer

Barbara Carnes

Alexandria, Virginia

ASTD Press is an internationally renowned source of insightful and practical information on workplace learning and performance topics, including training basics, evaluation and return on investment, instructional systems development, e-learning, leadership, and career development.

Ordering information: Books published by ASTD Press can be purchased by visiting ASTD's website at www.store.astd.org or by calling 800.628.2783 or 703.683.8100.

Library of Congress Control Number: 2009920429

ISBN-10: 1-56286-679-6
ISBN-13: 978-1-56286-679-2

ASTD Press Editorial Staff

Director: Dean Smith
Editorial Manager: Jacqueline Edlund-Braun
Senior Associate Editor: Tora Estep
Senior Associate Editor: Justin Brusino
Editorial Assistant: Victoria DeVaux

Copyeditor: Phyllis Jask
Indexer: April Davis
Proofreader: Kris Patenaude
Interior Design and Production: Kathleen Schaner
Cover Design: Katherine Warminsky
Cover Illustration: Shutterstock

Printed by Versa Press, Inc., East Peoria, Illinois, www.versapress.com

Dedication

To the memory of Dora Johnson, co-author and dear friend.
I miss her.

Contents

Preface

In my early years as a trainer, the training manager of a large company told me that when people go back to work after they have been to training, their supervisors more often than not say to them, "Forget everything you learned in training, now I'll tell you how we *really* do it!"

I recall when a woman came up to me at a conference and said I looked familiar to her. We talked about where we might have met each other and when she told me where she worked, I mentioned that I had conducted some training there several months earlier. She said, "Oh yes, I was in that class. It was a lot of fun!" I responded, "Great. How are you using what you learned?" She replied, "Let's see…what was the topic of the training?" She didn't even remember what the training was about!

How demoralizing is that? You work hard to put together and deliver a good training class, and it goes down the drain the minute trainees go back to their jobs.

Fellow trainer Dora Johnson and I met for coffee shortly after this incident, and, after whining and complaining about the issue, we decided to do some research about how to make training stick. We ended up making a lot of presentations to ASTD conferences and other training groups, and we wrote two books: *Making Training Stick* and *Making Training Stick: A Training Transfer Field Guide*, both of which have been very well received since they were first published. Between books, I did my PhD research and dissertation on the subject of training transfer. Dora passed away in 2005, and I decided to write this book by myself.

In the years since the first book was published, the workplace learning profession has become more aware of the issue of training transfer. Mary Broad and John Newstrom, Donald and James Kirkpatrick, and others have written books for the workplace learning practitioner community. The human resource development (HRD) academic community has published research studies on various aspects of training transfer, as it is called. Much more information is available today about activities and techniques that result in better transfer of training to the job, and about activities and techniques that don't.

Workplace learning professionals are busier today than they have ever been before. Budgets are tight. A need exists to bridge research with practice and to provide proven techniques that instructors, designers, and coaches can use easily and inexpensively.

I have used most of the techniques in this book in my own training and learning sessions. Many of my colleagues have used some of them as well.

Acknowledgments

Many thanks to Charles Albach, Belinda Brin, Karen Collins, and Margi Mainquist for providing helpful input and feedback on the book draft. Thanks to Cara Koen for help preparing the draft and web resources, to Larry Lanius for his photography, to the Center for Application of Information Technology at Washington University for use of their facility, and to the St. Louis Chapter of the American Society for Training & Development for the Sticky Session idea. Special thanks to the many friends and colleagues who continue to provide support and encouragement for my work on training transfer.

Chapter 1

Introduction:
How to Use This Book
to Your Best Advantage

What's in This Chapter:

This chapter will introduce

- important terms and concepts
- supporting research for the suggested techniques and a training transfer model
- training design and delivery recommendations.

This book can be used in a variety of ways depending on the readers' reading and learning styles, availability of time, and specific need. Although some may enjoy reading it cover to cover, others will want to use it as a reference, taking it off the shelf and reviewing it when making learning stick becomes top of mind. Here are some suggestions based on input from trainers who have used previous "stick" books:

- Read the first sections from beginning to end.
- Review the techniques—techniques to integrate education, or TIEs for short—with an eye for how each could be used.
- Set the book aside for future reference.

- Before designing, launching, refreshing, or conducting a learning event, pull the book off the shelf and review the TIEs. Choose the TIEs for before, during, and after the learning that are the best fit for the learning content, delivery platform, trainer, and organizational culture.
- Remember TIEs can be modified and adapted to fit specific needs and media.
- Consult www.MakeLearningStickResources.com for templates and other resources.

Terminology

The field of workplace learning is evolving. New terminology is replacing and augmenting more familiar terms. This book uses many terms in an effort to find words that are familiar to all readers. There is no significance as to which of the interchangeable terms is used at various points in the book.

Workplace learning, training, learning and development, and *human resource development (HRD)* refer to the organizational function(s) or department(s) focused on providing learning and other development opportunities to employees and, in some cases, to customers and vendors. These activities are often located in several different parts of the organization. For example, in many organizations the human resources department is responsible for legal compliance training, such as harassment prevention, as well as leadership, management, or supervisor skills, and other related types of learning. Frequently the operations area of an organization is involved with technical skills and safety training, and the sales and customer service areas oversee the learning for the sales staff and customer service representatives. Coaching may be provided within each of these areas or through specific departments throughout the organization.

The information and techniques in this book are relevant and useful regardless of the content of the learning—soft skills, compliance, technical, coaching, or sales/customer service.

Practitioners

Trainer, workplace learning professional, learning designer, presenter, instructor, and *coach* refer to practitioners who design, develop, write, conduct, facilitate, or coach learners in the workplace. Their role may be to facilitate learning and discovery, to present content to be learned, or to develop materials for this purpose. The background and professional preparation of these individuals vary. Some have academic degrees up to and including doctorates in areas such as HRD, training and development, adult learning, and instructional design. Others have degrees in psychology or business and through happenstance, serendipity, or progressive work assignments have become involved in workplace learning. Others in this field have preparation and experience in elementary and secondary education, coming to corporate training as a second career, while still others are subject matter experts (SMEs) in technical areas or sales who have become involved in workplace learning as a temporary or permanent job assignment. These individuals may work within an organization, as an external consultant, or as a third-party provider of learning.

Regardless of their background, education, and experience, some or all of their job responsibilities are to provide learning and development so that people can do their current and future jobs more effectively.

Ways to Deliver Learning

Training, learning event, program, class, course, and *coaching session* refer to the many ways learning is delivered to learners. Traditional classroom learning still has a prominent place in most organizations. Other modes of delivering learning are becoming more and more popular. E-learning, webinars, coaching sessions, and teleclasses fall within the scope of training, learning events, and programs, and within the scope of this book. To be considered a learning event as opposed to delivery of information, learners must interact with a trainer or coach or with the learning material. Although some content in this book may be more appropriate for one or more of these specific delivery modalities, most information is applicable to all of them.

Learners by Any Other Name

Participants, learners, coaching clients, and *trainees* are the individuals who participate in learning events. Hopefully they are also employees, customers, and vendors who apply what they learn to their jobs.

Training Transfer

Transfer of training is defined as the application on the job of knowledge, skills, and attitudes learned from training and the subsequent maintenance and use of them over a certain period of time.

Not Every Need Is a Training Need

It bears mentioning that not all perceived needs for training and coaching can in fact be resolved or addressed by training. This may account for a belief in some cases that training hasn't stuck. It may not have been a learning issue in the first place. As Robert Mager (1997) has impressed upon several generations of workplace learning professionals, if individuals can perform a skill "if their life depends on it," then it is not a training issue. Motivation and work environment may need to be adjusted. A trainee or coachee may not be willing to learn, and this should be addressed with him or her up front. An unwilling learner may blame the trainer or coach for the failure of learning to stick.

This book makes the assumption that training or coaching is an appropriate solution.

Background and Research

Much research on the topic of training transfer has been done since *Making Training Stick* and *Making Training Stick: A Training Transfer Field Guide* were published two decades ago. An overview of the most compelling research results follows, along with a model of the training transfer process.

Mary Broad and John Newstrom (1992) got the attention of the learning and development community when they introduced three time periods and three "pivotal roles" important for training transfer. Although based on limited survey research, their time/role matrices emphasized the importance of what happens to support training transfer before and after a training event, as well as the critical role the manager of the trainee plays in the transfer of training to the job. The three time periods mentioned are before, during, and after training. The pivotal roles are the manager, the trainee, and the trainer. Broad and Newstrom plotted these on a matrix and asked survey respondents, who were line managers and training practitioners, to rank the relative power of each time/role combination, with one being most important and nine being least important. The rankings follow in table 1-1.

Survey respondents then ranked the time/role combinations according to how frequently each was actually used, with one being most frequently used and nine being least frequently used (table 1-2).

A comparison of the most important time/role combinations with the most frequently used shows the greatest gaps between importance and use to be manager/before and manager/after (table 1-3).

Table 1-1. Most Powerful Time/Role Combinations

	Before	During	After
Manager	1	8	3
Trainer	2	4	9
Trainee	7	5	6

© Mary Broad. Used with permission

Table 1-2. Most Frequently Used Time/Role Combinations

	Before	During	After
Manager	5	6	9
Trainer	2	1	7
Trainee	8	3	4

© Mary Broad. Used with permission

Table 1-3. Most Frequently Used/Most Powerful

	Before	During	After
Manager	5/1	6/8	9/3
Trainer	2/2	1/4	7/9
Trainee	8/7	3/5	4/6

© Mary Broad. Used with permission

This information was interesting, but it was not empirical research—that is, it had not been verified or disproved by observation or experiment.

Many empirical research studies have been conducted since, and certain factors that play a significant role in the transfer of training have been identified. A need exists for more research on other factors that may also play a role. Most factors mentioned in this book are supported by multiple empirical research studies. These factors are grouped into three key categories: learner characteristics, organizational environment and support, and training design.

Figure 1-1 shows the training transfer process: before, during, and after the learning event. In their integrative review of research on training transfer, Burke and Hutchins (2007) identified factors associated with training transfer that are strongly supported by empirical research. I have placed these factors into a process model, in the style of previous process models (Baldwin and Ford, 1988; Kontoghiorghes, 2004; Machin and Fogerty, 2003).

Each of the factors in the model increases or accelerates the likelihood that transfer will occur. It should be noted, though, that in theory and in practice, some training transfer can occur regardless of each factor in the model. Even the worst training design, the most unsupportive environment, and learners without characteristics supportive of transfer may still result in the transfer of learning to the job. The more factors that are present, however, the more likely it is that more of the learning will be used on the job. The spiral arrows attempt to show this acceleration factor.

Here is a brief explanation of what is meant by each factor.

Learner Characteristics

Most workplace learning professionals think of the learner as a blank slate with lots of prior experience and knowledge but without other significant distinguishing qualities and characteristics. Yet considerable research indicates that trainees with certain characteristics are more likely to transfer their learning to their jobs. Hutchin and Burke's (2007) research survey of 170 workplace learning professionals found that the factors listed here are not widely recognized as being linked with training transfer, but research shows that they are.

Cognitive ability refers to general mental ability. People with higher cognitive ability are better able to retain the information and, therefore, transfer it to the workplace.

Self-efficacy is the belief an individual has about his or her ability to perform a particular task. Closely related to self-confidence, individuals with higher levels

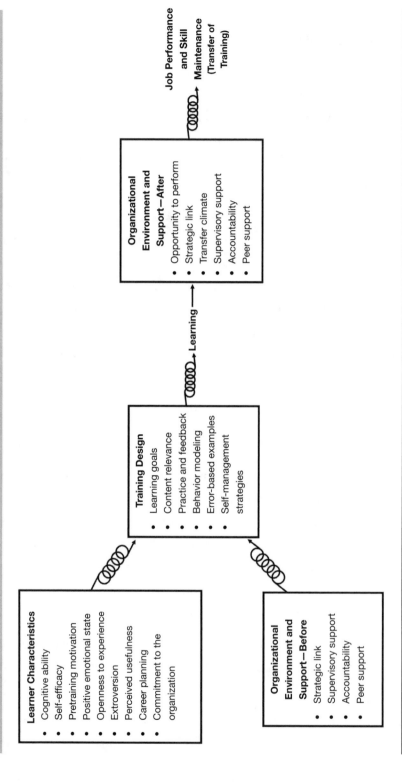

Figure 1-1. Training Transfer Process Model

Source: Compiled by Barbara Carnes for *Making Learning Stick* (ASTD, 2010)

of self-efficacy are more likely to believe that they can perform new skills and are more likely to use supportive behaviors so that they do transfer more skills learned in training to their jobs.

Pretraining motivation refers to the learner's interest before the training in learning the content and applying it to his or her job. Internal motivation to learn and apply the learning is more likely than external motivation to result in transfer. External motivators such as rewards and incentives have not been found to produce higher levels of transfer to the job. Performance appraisals are an aspect of the accountability factor, another trainee characteristic, and so are not an aspect of this factor.

Some learner personality characteristics were related to better training transfer. Learners with *positive mental emotional states* (commonly referred to as positive attitudes) were more likely to transfer learning to their job, and learners with negative mental emotional states were less likely to do so.

Trainees who were *open to new experiences* were found to be better able to capitalize on learning successes, to acquire skills faster, and to transfer the new skills to their jobs.

Extroversion, or rather the specific aspect of extroversion that involves the tendency to verbalize thoughts and feelings, is related to training transfer. This is not necessarily to say that only extroverts are likely to transfer learning to the job, however. Trainees who are more introverted benefit from having extroverts in training with them because the extroverts increase verbalization of strategies and applications, leading to more "cognitive sharing" so that all training participants benefit. A need exists for more research on this factor but it does seem reasonable.

Learners are more likely to transfer learning to the job when they believe that the *new skills will be useful to them in their jobs.* Put another way, when trainees *perceive* that they need to improve their job performance in areas related to the new skills being taught, they are more likely to transfer their training to the job.

Trainees with personal *career plans* that they update regularly are more likely to transfer their learning. They are able to see potential benefits of the training, long term as well as short term, more accurately.

Learners who identify with workplace groups (departments, work units) and are *committed to the organization* tend to transfer their learning to their jobs. There is a relationship between identification with workplace groups and the desire to gain and use new work-related knowledge.

Training Design

Instructional designers and trainers have intuitively known that certain elements of a good training design lead to better learning in the classroom. Research studies indicate that these elements have also consistently been found to lead to higher levels of training transfer to the job.

Objectives or goals for the learning that are explicitly communicated to trainees show them what performance is expected. When these are present in the learning, there are higher levels of training transfer. When trainees receive the objectives in advance of the training, they are likely to have even higher levels of transfer.

When the learning *content is relevant* and specific to the trainee's job duties, it is more likely to be applied to the job. The goals, materials, and skill practices should be adapted not only for the industry and the employer but also for specific job titles/duties.

When participants have opportunities to practice skills in the training and *receive feedback* on their practice, they are more likely to transfer the training to their jobs. Specifically, mental rehearsal ("what would you do if" scenarios) and behavioral practice strategies (role playing) have the strongest correlations with transfer. Distributing practice sessions throughout the training rather than concentrating them in one part of the learning event also results in higher levels of transfer.

Behavior modeling, that is, showing participants the desired performance or behavior either via audiovisual or in-person demonstration, enhances transfer.

Transfer is increased even more when key aspects of the demonstrated performance are described to the trainees.

Error-based examples are the flip side of behavior modeling. In an error-based example, participants are shown ineffective behaviors or are shown demonstrations of desired and undesired performance mixed together. Trainees who participate in these types of demonstrations are more likely to transfer their learning to the job.

Certain *self-management instructional strategies* have been found to increase training transfer. Two main types of strategies have the most research support: goal setting and the self-management model called relapse prevention. With both strategies, close to the conclusion of the training, participants envision how they will use the skills learned and develop a strategy for doing so.

Organizational Environment and Support—Before and After Training

Before and after training, the support of key individuals and the overall climate or culture of the organization, including certain organizational practices, are linked with higher levels of training transfer.

Trainees who understand how the *strategic direction* and goals of the organization are linked with the training content seem to be more likely to use on the job what they have learned in training. More research is needed on this factor, though.

Trainee *supervisors who show their support* for the training both before and afterward influence trainees' transfer of skills to the job. Certain specific activities—discussing the learning with the trainee, participating in the training or a shortened version of it, and providing encouragement and coaching—have been shown to lead to better transfer. Other supervisor activities may also play a role and are being researched.

Accountability refers to the extent that management, including the trainee's supervisor, other members of management, and/or the organizational culture, expects learners to use what they learn and holds them responsible for doing so. This can be accomplished through performance expectations and reviews, requiring learners to report afterward on their experience and their learning, and, conversely, providing sanctions for failure to use learned skills on the job. More research is needed on this factor, however.

Trainees' peers exert a strong influence on transfer of skills and knowledge. Networking with peers prior to a learning event helps them understand the value of the learning and specific ways it can be used on the job. Sharing ideas afterward about course content, applications, challenges, and successes exerts strong influence on trainees' use of skills and knowledge on the job.

The *opportunity to perform new skills* soon after returning from training has a strong influence on whether trainees consistently use their learning. What we use, we remember. Several studies have found that this factor is the strongest transfer influence, and its absence is the greatest impediment to transfer.

A *climate* within the organization that supports training transfer is more likely to produce individuals who transfer their learning to their jobs. Cues and reminders, such as job aids, strategically placed posters, newsletter reminders, and so on, prompt trainees to use their new skills. Feedback and encouragement provided by supervisor and peers, positive consequences for using skills correctly, and remedial assistance when the skills are not used also play a part in a positive transfer climate.

Future research will undoubtedly reveal other factors that influence training transfer. Some research has been conducted on motivation to learn and motivation to transfer as well as extrinsic versus intrinsic motivation. More research is needed, however, to determine the exact role these factors may play in training transfer. Overlearning and cognitive overload show some relationship to training transfer but more research is needed here as well.

Locus of control—that is, the extent to which participants believe they have control of their own destiny and outcomes—has been found in some studies to be related to transfer of training; however, other studies have found no relationship.

Active learning design, conscientiousness as a trainee characteristic, and technological support are also factors that may play a part in training transfer and require additional research.

All of the research mentioned here has been focused on classroom learning events, yet more and more learning is being delivered through coaching and virtually through e-learning, webinars, and teleclasses. Little if any research has been conducted on how these types of learning events influence the transfer of learning to the job. This is also an important area for future research.

The techniques in this book are, for the most part, based on the described model of training transfer and the research that supports it. However, even though the model is based on classroom learning events, most of the techniques in this book can be adapted and used with e-learning, webinars, teleclasses, and coaching sessions.

Chapter 2

TIEs That Bind

What's in This Chapter:

This chapter offers

- an explanation of techniques to integrate education (TIE)
- access information to download examples, samples, and new TIEs from the Internet
- a list of the TIEs in this and other books.

This story has touched trainers for more than two decades:

Once upon a time in the land of human resource development (HRD) there was an organization that relied on the work of participant bears to produce goods and services, which created money to pay the taxes that kept the land healthy and well. The organization thrived, the bears were paid well for their work, and the land prospered. The bears worked exceptionally well together. Each knew his or her job, how each job related to the others, and why each job was important to the overall vision of the organization.

Also in this organization were trainer bees. The bees were very effective in their jobs of assessing needs and developing, delivering, and evaluating outstanding training programs. Each bee also worked well with others, knew his or her job, how it related to others, and why that job was important to the overall mission of the organization.

Everything was going along just fine in the land of HRD until something new appeared—change. Change that required the bears to be trained in a new production/service technique very quickly. The trainer bees assessed the need, designed an exceptional training program, and trained the first 50 participant bears on the new technique. The end of program evaluations were outstanding. Three weeks later the bees checked back with the bears to see how they were using the new techniques.

The bees found that some participant bears were using the new techniques, but others had returned to their old way of doing things. The bees knew it was critical that *all* bears use the technique, so the head bee called a staff meeting to design something that would cause the participant bears to implement the training back on the worksite.

The head bee started the meeting by explaining the situation and outlining the task for the meeting. They needed to find something to help the bears remember what they had learned in training so they would use the new techniques on the job.

The bees talked about threats, but discarded that idea because they knew it would only cause resistance. They discussed leaving the participant bears alone and being satisfied with the low success rate. They rejected that idea immediately because they knew they could solve this problem and were not willing to give up so soon. They thought about requiring the bears to use the techniques through assignments, but said no to this idea. It was too much like school, and the bees knew that the bears would resist.

Finally, they decided to look further for techniques that would increase the use of the new skill. They agreed that the techniques needed to be

- a product of the training program—directly related to what was included in the learning
- enticing to the participant bears
- pleasant and enjoyable
- something the bears could use and want
- a way to connect the training outcomes to the job.

The trainer bees thought and pondered. "What is a product of our efforts, enticing, pleasant, desired by bears, and sticky?" they asked.

"Ah ha!" said the bees. "Honey. Honey is a product of our efforts, enticing, pleasant, and desired by bears, and certainly is sticky. We will coat each of our training sessions with a special honey—techniques to integrate education—so that the bears will want to take the learning back to their jobs."

They tried it. The participant bears loved it, and, most important, they started using what they had learned back on their jobs.

And they all worked happily ever after.

What Is a TIE?

TIE is an abbreviation for *technique to integrate education.* In the story, the TIE is the honey that the trainer bees made, which the participant bears liked, that made the training stick.

This book, like the two before it, contains techniques to integrate education, which workplace learning professionals and human resource practitioners can use before, during, and after learning events to make the learning stick. Although some TIEs may lend themselves to particular types of training content (soft skills, technical skills, and so on), most TIEs can be used with any type of content. Likewise, whereas some TIEs may lend themselves to certain types of learning delivery, most TIEs can be used with a variety of delivery means—classroom, e-learning, webinar, teleclass, or coaching session.

TIEs are easy to use with new learning programs and with already-developed training. The purpose of each TIE is to increase the transfer of the participants' learning to their jobs so the learning sticks. All of the TIEs are based on research and are low cost. The description of each TIE contains step-by-step instructions, the downside when the TIE might not be effective, variations, and other TIEs that could easily be combined with it. The detailed instructions will be a quick reference to minimize prep time for the workplace learning professional. Use the TIEs in this book as is, adapt them, or use them as a springboard to create new TIEs.

To summarize, TIEs are

- step-by-step instructions to make learning stick
- easy to use
- low cost or no cost
- used with new or existing learning
- used regardless of training topic
- adaptable for classroom, e-learning, webinar, teleclass, or coaching session.

There is no claim to originality of these TIEs. Some have originated with other trainers; others have been used under different names. Most TIEs, however, have not previously been linked with making the learning stick.

Many TIEs can be combined. The most likely combinations are suggested at the end of each TIE description. A few examples of forms are provided as well. More samples and examples with downloadable forms can be found at www .MakeLearningStickResources.com. Be sure to share your examples of how you use the TIEs, too.

Original Techniques to Integrate Education

The following TIEs were originally introduced in *Making Training Stick* and were added to and expanded in *Making Training Stick: A Training Transfer Field Guide.* They are summarized here for your reference.

Acknowledging. Most people don't handle compliments very well. When someone pays a compliment, most people say thank you; some don't even do that. Many times they don't internalize the compliment. Yet acknowledgments are more effective than punishments or negative consequences in getting people to change their behavior. There are many different ways to acknowledge participants when they succeed in making training stick.

Action Planning. Often participants are excited about how they will use what they have learned. During the training they may come up with all sorts of ways to use it. After they have returned to work, however, they often report that they got involved in daily activities and perhaps a crisis or two, and forgot about how they said they were going to use the training. Engaging participants in an action plan at the end of the training will help them remember to apply their learning and make it stick.

Affirmations. The Bible talks about them, weight loss programs use them, positive mental attitude gurus recommend them. For thousands of years, people have reported amazing results from them. An affirmation is a positive statement in the present tense that describes a desired result as if it were already true. Repeated several times daily, an affirmation convinces the subconscious mind that the affirmation statement is true. Once the subconscious begins to believe the statement, it works to make it a reality. If it works for things like weight loss and positive mental attitude, why not training? Why not stress management, communication skills, software system skills, and many other learning topics?

***Aha!* Sheet.** Participants are encouraged to write key learnings—their "*ahas*"—as these occur during the training. A separate aha! sheet is given to participants so they can write key learnings and points to remember, and the "so what"—how they can use each of them.

Alumni Day. School reunions are usually high-energy, high-anticipation events. Why not training reunions? Don't wait 10 or 20 years before having a training reunion, though. Plan an Alumni Day for all graduates of a class or graduates of just one class. Schedule it to follow a current class. Involve graduates in the current class, as facilitators or guest speakers. Allow graduates to rekindle old bonds and in the process reinforce their learning.

Board Games. A little healthy competition will increase interest and participation during the training. When used afterward, board games provide a fun way to reinforce the learning and cue trainees to use what they learned. Even people who haven't attended the training may want to play a round or two. Strategically placed in work or break areas, people can play a board game on breaks or during workday lulls. Developing a content-specific board game needn't be difficult or time consuming. Existing games can often be adapted.

Coaching. The process of coaching has become a popular means of preparing individuals with high potential for greater responsibilities and also a means of helping turn around substandard performance. The coach may be someone external to the organization, someone from another part of the organization, or a supervisor. Coaching as a TIE focuses on specific skills learned in training and is conducted by the trainee's supervisor, the trainer, or both.

Coloring Book. The old saying goes "a picture is worth a thousand words." Most people are better able to recall a picture of something than a description of it. The act of drawing a picture or sketch also solidifies recall and helps the person who is doing the drawing clarify his or her learning. The act of coloring with crayons or markers can also serve to help participants reflect on what they have learned and how they will put it to use. Use a coloring book TIE during training as a break from more routine activities, or use it after training as a reinforcement.

Contracts. Contracts mean commitment. Malcolm Knowles (1975), generally acknowledged as the father of adult education, introduced the learning contract as a way to build participant commitment to learn. The TIE transfer contract in a similar way builds commitment to take the learning back to the job. An important aspect of the transfer contract, as with any contract, is commitment from all parties: the trainee, to use what has been learned; the manager, to assist as needed; the trainer, to be available for questions and to reinforce.

Critical Incidents. Do people remember times when things went well or when everything seemed to go wrong? Experience has found that they remember when things went wrong. Why not harness these memories to build commitment to do things right? Participants describe an incident, which is then used as a discussion vehicle to generate analysis and commitment to use new skills and behavior to avoid similar outcomes in the future. This is also a good way to gather examples for the next time the program is presented.

Exercises. A generally accepted training technique, exercises are used often in a training program so participants can practice what they are learning. TIE exercises are used after the program has ended to help participants remember and continue to learn. Short activities that are similar to those in the training program allow the participants to reconnect with the training experiences and to identify and alert the workplace learning professional to any learning or skill gaps.

Intentions. Offer someone a $1 million cashier's check, and most likely he or she would want it. What if he or she had to give over $10,000 to get the check? Would he or she still want it? What if there were only 24 hours to get the money? And the money had to be in cash? Saying yes to each question is setting an intention—being willing to do whatever it takes to get the result. This same process can be used to help learners set intentions to use skills learned in training and to overcome any obstacles that may get in the way.

Job Aids and Reminders. Pocket cards, monitor stickers, and hang tags are just a few examples of job aids and reminders to help trainees remember skills learned in training. This in-a-nutshell information is especially helpful if the trainee needs to use the skill or information only occasionally. Reminders can be given out during training or sent out afterward.

Letter to Self. Trainees usually leave training with the best intentions to begin using what they have learned. They may even talk about how they plan to apply the new skills and knowledge. But then they discover the alligators waiting for them back on the job and suddenly clearing out the swamp takes priority over applying their training. Then one day an envelope shows up in their own handwriting. Most likely they do not remember writing to themselves in the training program a few weeks before. But there it is, in their own writing: what they plan to do, what obstacles might come up, and what they can do to overcome them.

Newsletter. A well-planned, well-written newsletter transforms the training experience from a one-time event to an ongoing learning experience. A joke, notes from other trainees, and tidbits of information can be combined into a short-and-sweet piece of easy reading that reinforces the learning. Sounds like a lot of work? It doesn't have to be. Shorter is better.

Pat on the Back. A pat on the back card is given to the participant when his or her supervisor or trainer observes him or her on the job using the skills learned in training. The card can be handed out spontaneously, or as part of a planned after-training skill observation. Many variations include kudos cards and blue ribbons.

Personalized Objectives. In addition to the published training objectives, participants add their own learning objectives for their training. Best done before the training begins, trainees are asked to use the same language or wording scheme as the provided objectives. After reviewing the published objectives, trainees are asked to add one or two of their own and send to the trainer before the beginning of the class.

Propaganda. Buttons, candy jars, pens, letter openers…the list of specialty advertising items can go on and on. Marketing and sales people know that when people see and use these types of items, they tend to remember the message printed on them—not only on the conscious level but on the subconscious level as well. So save those pens left over from the last sales meeting. Develop a slogan or tagline that captures what trainees should remember. Choose from the many item options available from specialty advertising dealers or your organization's own advertising department. Why use these gimmicks? Because most people like them, and what they like they tend to keep around and use. When they use them, the training is reinforced and is more likely to stick.

Pulse Check. The trainer stops periodically throughout training and asks key questions about what participants are learning and how they will apply their learning to their jobs. Pulse check cards can be used so participants can review their pulse check responses as reminders at the end of the training and afterward on the job.

Questionnaire. TIE questionnaires are short and to the point. The reason for sending them to trainees before or after training is not necessarily to get answers, although this information may be helpful, too. The reason for sending pre- and posttraining questionnaires to trainees is to set the psychological stage for the learning beforehand and to reinforce it afterward.

Report Card. Participants and/or their supervisors are given a report card or grade report form similar to those used in school. The card contains a list of skills to be practiced after training and a check box for A, B, C, and so on, or a field to write in the grade. Once back on the job, the participant, supervisor, or both fill in the grades as the skills are used. Offer a prize for returning the completed card.

Support Groups. Being the sole subject matter expert in the training class and afterward is often a burden. Trainees are often able to provide support to one another after the learning to share what is working and what is not. Frequently support group members (or pairs) have a better understanding of what actually goes on in the trenches than the trainer does. Whether the support groups meet regularly or just once or twice after training, whether they meet virtually or in person, whether they meet in a group or in pairs, or whether the instructor attends or not, sharing successes and helping each other overcome obstacles increase the likelihood that trainees will remember and use their learning on the job.

Teleconferencing. A posttraining teleconference can take the form of adding to material covered in class, discussing challenges and successes (much like a support group), or using a tool to reinforce accountability to use newly learned skills on the job. It differs from a teleclass because the purpose is to reinforce the learning so that it sticks and is applied on the job.

Transfer Certificate. Traditional training certificates acknowledge participation in the training and are given to participants at the conclusion of the event. The transfer certificate is given after the supervisor or trainer observes the participant using one or more of the skills learned in training in the course of doing his or her regular work.

The Ziegarnik Effect. Named after a Russian psychologist, this little-known effect is about interruptions and closure. When people get closure on a thought or learning—that is, when the content has been thoroughly covered, questions have been answered, and skills practiced—they tend to mentally file it in their memory bank to be retrieved when and if needed. However, when people do not get closure and when they are interrupted in their learning, their subconscious returns to the topic, and brings it up to the conscious level at various times for further thought and reflection. To get the Ziegarnik effect, stop before finishing a point or instruction. Don't allow closure.

Overview of TIEs in This Book

The TIEs in this book provide more techniques that can be used before, during, and after learning events and can be used by trainer, manager, and participant. Table 2-1 and short descriptions below provide a quick, easy overview. Each TIE is explained in depth in chapter 3.

Table 2-1. TIE Summary

TIE	Before	During	After
Boss Briefing/Debriefing	X		X
Podcasts	X		X
Protect Participants	X	X	
Strategy Link	X	X	X
Can-Do Attitude	X	X	X
The Proof's in the Pudding	X		
Seeds	X	X	
Apples	X	X	
Target Objectives	X	X	
Color in the Classroom	X	X	
Credit Cards			X
Trainees as Teachers		X	X
Success Stories and Lessons Learned			X
Mind Sweep		X	
Relapse Prevention		X	X
Use It or Lose It Checklist		X	X
Training Buddies	X	X	X
Sticky Sessions			X
Screen Saver			X
Webpage	X		X

Boss Briefing/Debriefing. Communication from the trainee's manager or supervisor before and after the training helps the trainee understand the importance of the learning and how it will help him or her do the job better. Whether the communication is face to face, by phone, or by email, this short communication can make a big difference.

Podcasts. Trainees can download these short sound or sound and video files from an email or a website before or after the learning event to reinforce and add tips for using what has been learned.

Protect Participants. Learners who are distracted from the learning by what is happening back on the job don't learn as well or as much as if they gave their full attention to their learning—even on breaks. These tips will help participants stay focused.

Strategy Link. When participants understand how the learning event links with the business strategy of the organization, they use more of what they learn. There are many different, time-efficient ways to communicate this linkage throughout the learning event.

Can-Do Attitude. When trainees believe they can learn and use a skill, they are more likely to do it. Belief creates action. Use these strategies and tactics before, during, and after training to boost trainees' confidence and belief in their ability.

The Proof's in the Pudding. Using comments and testimonials from previous program participants as part of the class description and registration information is a powerful way to build positive expectations and to help those enrolled understand the benefits of participating in the learning.

Seeds. Having the right mix of trainees in a classroom learning event affects all participants' learning. Seed classes with talkative, extroverted learners to get the best training transfer.

Apples. Participants whose attitudes and motivation do not support the learning can also affect all participants in the class. Spread them out or contain them to maximize the learning for others.

Target Objectives. Ask participants to prioritize the objectives beforehand or at the beginning of the learning event. Reviewing and interacting with the objectives helps learners focus and provides valuable input to the trainer as well.

Color in the Classroom. Certain colors elicit certain emotional responses in most people. Use colors in the classroom and in the materials to support specific learning goals.

Credit Cards. Reinforcement is one of the most effective, and most researched, methods for changing human—and even animal—behavior. Awarding credit cards in different forms is a way to reinforce the use of skills learned when they occur on the job.

Trainees as Teachers. One way to learn is to teach the material. Enlist trainees to teach parts of the material to their fellow participants, or ask them to return to a later class to teach some, even a small portion, of it.

Success Stories and Lessons Learned. Once participants get back to their jobs and begin using their new skills, they have valuable information to share. Implementing a discussion forum, face-to-face brown bag lunch series, or other means to help participants share what is working and what is not facilitates this important information sharing.

Mind Sweep. This Gestalt-type technique helps participants clear their minds so they can fully focus on their learning without mental distractions and preoccupations with work, home, or family issues.

Relapse Prevention. Engage participants in a discussion with specific questions that help them anticipate obstacles to using what they have learned and how to overcome them. This structured discussion technique has been used successfully in other types of behavior management programs, and it works equally well for training transfer.

Use It or Lose It Checklist. Participants complete this checklist at the end of the learning event, and it becomes a quick reference once they return to the job—it encourages them to immediately begin practicing and using their new skills.

Training Buddies. Assign or allow trainees to choose learning partners before, at the beginning, or at the end of a learning event. Buddies provide support, input, feedback, and accountability for learning and then for applying skills on the job.

Sticky Sessions. Short sessions after the learning event facilitated by the trainer provide reinforcement of the learning content and opportunities for application discussions in more depth than often takes place in the training itself.

Screen Saver. A sentence or phrase that comes up on a trainee's screen saver provides reinforcement for the learning and a reminder to apply the learning to the job.

Webpage. A resource page with articles, links, and other information as well as posts from participants provides a way for the learning to continue and serves as a support mechanism for applying the learning to the job.

What's Coming Up

To make learning stick, the bees decided they needed to develop techniques to increase the use of the bears' new skills. The honey—techniques to integrate education, or TIEs—was just what they needed to get the bears excited to use their newfound learning on the job.

The purpose of each TIE is to increase the transfer of the participants' learning to their jobs so the learning sticks. Many TIEs can be used or adapted and applied to different learning environments—classroom, coaching session, tele-class, webinar, e-learning—with great success.

Ready for more? Each of the TIEs described in this chapter are discussed more in depth in chapter 3.

Chapter 3

20 Easy-to-Use, Low-Cost Techniques to Transfer Learning

What's in This Chapter:

This chapter includes the following TIEs:

- Boss Briefing/Debriefing: Use Manager to Encourage Application on the Job
- Podcasts: Listen-and-Stick Learning
- Protect Participants: Reduce Distractions to Keep Focus
- Strategy Link: Connect Organizational Strategy to Specific Training
- Can-Do Attitude: Support Success and Positive Outcomes
- The Proof's in the Pudding: Use Testimonials to Build Support and Positive Expectations
- Seeds: Plant Extroverts to Germinate Application Participation
- Apples: Minimize the Influence of Some Participants

- Target Objectives: Involve, Personalize, Engage
- Color in the Classroom: Support Your Content a Different Way
- Credit Cards: Reward Success in Tangible and Spendable Ways
- Trainees as Teachers: Give Participants a Turn to Teach and Engage
- Success Stories and Lessons Learned: Encourage Participants to Share
- Mind Sweep: Clear Minds of Distractions That Block Learning
- Relapse Prevention: Facilitate a Powerful Discussion with Proven Results
- Use It or Lose It Checklist: Commit Participants to After-Training Action
- Training Buddies: Encourage Peer Learning Support Before, During, and After Training
- Sticky Sessions: Drive Learning Home with After-Training Application Meetings
- Screen Saver: Provide Desktop Messaging for Real-Time Reminders
- Webpage: Keep Learning Alive with Resources and Support

The 20 techniques along with how-to explanations are all arranged in the same order beginning with a brief explanation and overview followed by step-by-step instructions. Next, you are given the downsides of using that particular technique and some interesting variations to try. Each TIE offers more samples and examples with downloadable forms at www.MakeLearningStick Resources.com. Be sure to share your examples of how you use the TIEs, too.

Boss Briefing/Debriefing: Use Manager to Encourage Application on the Job

Who: trainer/trainee's supervisor
When: before/after
Media: face-to-face, e-learning, webinar, teleclass, coaching

Few workplace learning professionals argue the importance of the boss or trainee's supervisor in making learning stick to the job. The trainee's supervisor can link and communicate how specific skills, techniques, and knowledge can be applied to a participant's particular job. The trainee's supervisor can set the stage for training by building positive expectations and reducing distractions and work expectations during training. Afterward, the trainee's supervisor can provide or assist with opportunities to use what has been learned in training. The trainee's supervisor can model the skills being taught. And the trainee's supervisor can support and assist with postlearning challenges as well as celebrate successes.

Although many bosses and supervisors are fully aware of the critical role they play in making learning stick, others need assistance and reminders to perform their role. Even if the trainee's supervisor does not use the skills being taught, if he or she acknowledges this to the trainee and also discusses the value of using the skills, research shows the learning is still more likely to stick.

Trainer—or learning and development department—communication with the trainee's supervisor should specify as directly as possible what the supervisor is expected to do and say before and after one of his or her employees participates in a learning event. Many organizations hold supervisors accountable through performance objectives and reviews for making certain their employees participate in learning and are supported before and afterward.

1. Determine specifically what the trainee's supervisor should do and say to support the learning. Depending on the learning content and the variation in participants' job titles, customizing what specific supervisors are asked to do and say may be necessary. It may be helpful to have a conversation with

a few supervisors or with senior managers to get ideas for possible ways to support the training and messages to send before and after training.

2. Investigate—if you don't know—any accountabilities that may be in place for the trainees' supervisors, such as their performance expectations for supporting their employees' training.

3. Make a list of what the trainee's supervisor should do and say before and after the learning event. Be specific.

Before the learning event, supervisors could

- communicate with the participant about the learning event: what will be covered and why it is important for his or her job and for the organization's mission and strategy. This communication can be via face-to-face meeting, phone meeting, voicemail, or even email. Two-way communication is preferable to one-way so that trainee questions and concerns can be addressed, but any pretraining communication is better than none.

- familiarize themselves with the learning content. If they have participated in this or similar learning previously, a quick review of the materials would be helpful. Otherwise, provide a short verbal or written summary.

- check on their employee's workload. Address any deadlines, projects, or other work that may interfere with full participation in the learning event. Reschedule training if necessary.

During the learning event, supervisors could

- protect employees from interruptions and distractions as much as possible.

After the learning event supervisors could

- debrief with the participant on what was learned and how to apply it on the job

- help the participant find opportunities to use newly learned skills and knowledge right away

- develop and communicate accountabilities for using what has been learned: establish check-in dates, establish progress timelines, or include using new skills in the development plan portion of the performance review.

The trainer should then communicate to the trainee's supervisor what is expected of both the supervisor and the participant enrolled in upcoming learning (see figure 3-1). Consider getting an "introduction" from a senior manager.

After the training, the trainer should again communicate to the participant's supervisor what participants have learned along with a customized list of what is expected of the supervisor at this point.

Figure 3-1. Sample Letter to Supervisor

	New Message	
Send Chat Attach Address Fonts Colors Save As Draft		
To:		
Cc:		
Subject:		

Dear Mike,

As you know, your employee, Tina Trainee, will participate in Introduction to Management next week. Attached is a short summary of what will be covered in the three-day class.

To make the most of our company's investment in Tina's training, would you please go over the following with her before the training begins next Tuesday:

- Good management skills make a huge difference in our company's success and profitability.
- Managers affect productivity, worker satisfaction, willingness to continue to work here, quality of our products, and much more.
- The company's goal this year is to become the market leader and to do this we're going to need skilled supervisors.

Also to minimize interruptions and distractions, would you please talk with Tina about voicemail and email coverage? We have found that people learn much more and do better in training when they are not required to check voicemail and email, except at lunch.

If you have any questions or concerns, please contact me.

Thanks,

Trainer Jack

Downside

This TIE may not be as effective as it could be if

- the importance of the learning and how it fits with the organization's mission and strategy have not been communicated and are not understood by the trainee's supervisor
- the supervisor does not have a clear understanding of the training content and how it can be applied to the trainee's job
- the participant's supervisor does not understand the many options for one-way and two-way communication with the employee about his or her learning. Consider writing a "script" for supervisors to use.

Variations

- A senior manager could communicate with the employee, instead of or in addition to communication from the participant's immediate supervisor.
- Trainees could be asked or told to initiate discussions with their supervisors before and/or after the learning event. They might also be asked to report back to the trainer the results of the conversation.
- The trainer/coach and the trainee's supervisor, with employee involvement, could jointly determine desired outcomes and decide on a feedback plan so that the supervisor regularly provides feedback to the coach on progress.
- Work with employees to determine desired outcomes and decide on a plan for feedback with the coach.
- Hold a pretraining event (face-to-face, webinar, e-learning, luncheon) especially for the trainees' supervisors. This event could contain both a shortened version of the learning content and instructions for how to support the trainee before and afterward.
- Provide a web link to a short e-learning content summary with instructions to the trainee's supervisor for how to support the trainee and the training.

Combine With

Target Objectives, Podcasts, Protect Participants, Strategy Link, Use It or Lose It Checklist

Podcasts: Listen-and-Stick Learning

Who: trainer/ trainee's supervisor
When: before/after
Media: face-to-face, e-learning, webinar, teleclass, coaching

Today's learners are on the move. It's hard enough to get them to attend a face-to-face learning event or e-learning program; it's harder yet to engage them before or after a learning event, when they are immersed in their job—and their lives. Listening to an audio file can be easily integrated into a learner's workday, commute, exercise, and even household duties. Whether these files are played on the computer or on a portable listening device, they provide a convenient way to prepare participants for what they are about to learn and/or to provide follow-up information, guidance, and reinforcement after training. Video files can be used in much the same way, although playback opportunities are more limited.

Podcasts can also be used with trainees' supervisors and other centers of influence. A brief audio file can be used to sell the supervisor on the value of the training and its importance for the trainees' job performance. A recap of the learning content can be provided to the trainee's supervisor either before or after the learner participates in the learning program. Specific pretraining and posttraining steps and activities for the trainee's supervisor to take to support the learning can be spelled out (see the Boss Briefing/Debriefing TIE).

Making an audio file is as easy as talking into a recording device or personal computer, or more sophisticated studio-recorded features can be used. Making a video file is as easy as making home videos with a camcorder, or more sophisticated features can be used here as well.

1. Assess the technology of the audience. Most workplace learners access audio and video files at their desktop computer (80 percent according to one survey) so they don't necessarily need to have a portable listening device. It helps, though, to have an idea of what devices people have and how they are most likely to use them for this purpose. Be sure learners have sound cards on their computers. Although a sound card is a

standard feature on home computers, some organizations do not include sound cards as part of their standard computer configurations.

2. Determine the attention span of the intended audience. How long should this podcast be? This is especially important when the intended audience is supervisors who have not participated in the learning event. The length of podcasts can range from a three- to four-minute sound bite to longer programs of 20–30 minutes.

3. Decide on a format. One person talking into a microphone is an easy format. It can also be boring. Two-person interviews provide variety and interest. Interview a senior leader about why the learning is important to the organization's strategy. Interview a past participant about how he or she has implemented the learning—challenges as well as successes. Other formats to consider that are easy to produce include radio talk shows, call-in shows (with dummy call-ins), and two-person radio show moderators. Somewhat more complicated but worth the effort are quiz or game shows. Listen to talk radio and public radio shows for ideas.

4. Draft an outline, not a word-for-word script. This approach makes for a more natural delivery style, which is more pleasing to the listener. Practice out loud what will be said. Remember, it doesn't have to be perfect. Major blunders can be edited. Minor mistakes are forgivable and make the program sound more natural and real.

5. Set up the technology. Software for recording and simple editing is available for free or a low cost by searching for "podcast software" or similar search terms. Invest in an external microphone rather than trying to use the computer's internal microphone. The better sound quality is worth the small cost. Inexpensive external microphones that are for sale where computer accessories are sold usually provide adequate sound quality.

6. Try a sample recording. Plug in the mike and practice the content delivery either in its entirety or a portion of it. Play it back. When you're satisfied with the sound quality and the process, you're ready to do the real thing. If the recording will be a video recording, be sure to check lighting and background.

7. Once the recording has been finished, upload and save it into the software in one of several file formats. Edit as needed.
8. Store the file on any computer, email it, place a link to it on a webpage, or insert it into an e-learning program or graphic presentation.
9. Distribute or post it.

Downside

This TIE may not be as effective as it could be if

- trainees and other intended audiences do not have appropriate equipment—at least a sound card on their computer and perhaps a mobile listening device
- the podcast program is longer than the attention span of most listeners—trainees and/or their managers; break longer content into shorter programs
- the podcast program is boring
- the subject of the podcast is not relevant for the learners or supervisors
- the podcast content is more appropriate for two-way dialogue than one-way communication.

Variations

- Include a link to the podcast in a post-event follow-up note to trainees and to their supervisors.
- Use a podcast as a tool to describe a learning event. Include the podcast file in the learning program description and preregistration information.
- Play a podcast in a classroom or webinar learning event to add variety. The file link can be inserted into a presentation slide.
- Put the program on a CD and distribute to learners at the conclusion or after the learning event.

Combine With

Boss Briefing/Debriefing, Strategy Link, Can-Do Attitude, Trainees as Teachers, Relapse Prevention, Use It or Lose It Checklist, Webpage

Protect Participants: Reduce Distractions to Keep Focus

Who: trainer/manager
When: before/during
Media: face-to-face, e-learning, webinar, teleclass, coaching

The trainee is engrossed in the learning event. Then his or her phone vibrates or rings, someone comes up to his or her desk, a new email arrives, or someone appears at the door with an urgent message. Off the trainee goes to solve the problem, avert the crisis, or deal with the issue. Whether he or she quickly steps outside the classroom door to take a call, briefly navigates away from a webinar, or his or her departure takes him or her even farther away from the learning, focus has been lost.

Another scenario: The trainee picks up messages during a break, or takes a break from an e-learning program, and receives news that continues to occupy his or her mind once the learning event has resumed. Self-interruptions are often even more compelling than interruptions caused by other people.

Whether the interruption is caused by someone else or is self-imposed, it takes a person a little over a minute to reorient and refocus after a distraction. This may not seem like a lot of time, but key pieces of information and discussion can take place in a 60-second timeframe.

The realities of today's work environments require workplace learning professionals to be flexible and tolerant when participants are called out of training. Too often, however, the parties involved—interrupter, "interruptee," and trainer—don't fully understand the consequences of the interruption. Protect participants from themselves. Protect them from others. With so many possible distractions and with trainees so accustomed to multiple stimuli and many irons in the fire, they often unconsciously look for ways to distract themselves.

Training transfer research has found that when participants stay focused on the learning—even during breaks—they retain more of the content and show higher levels of transfer to their jobs. Transfer levels are lowest for trainees who use their breaks to go back to their desks and catch up on work. Checking messages on breaks is one thing, using breaks as mini–work sessions is quite another.

1. Help the trainee and his or her supervisor prepare for the trainee's involvement in the training and absence from the job. Provide plenty of advance notice of the training. If the trainee's supervisor typically sends him or her to training, communicate with the supervisor well in advance and suggest the trainee have outgoing voicemail and email messages indicating he or she will be in training for the specified time period. Although it may be necessary for the trainee to remain available for emergencies and other unexpected things that may come up, it is reasonable to ask others to expect a response after the training has concluded.

2. Provide a short pretraining checklist for the trainee and his or her supervisor that includes voicemail and email coverage as well as workload expectations during training (see figure 3-2). Explain that for the trainee to get the most from the investment in training, he or she should not be interrupted by phone or in person except in case of an emergency that can't wait until the end of the learning event. Also mention that laptops are discouraged because they are a distraction not only to the participant but to other participants.

3. At the beginning of the webinar, e-learning, or classroom training, ask participants to set their phones to voicemail and turn their cell phones completely off, not on vibrate. In the classroom, if laptops are present, ask that they be used for note taking only, to support the best possible learning and as a courtesy to fellow participants. Monitor laptop use. If a laptop is being used for other purposes, discretely ask the participant to stop. (Reading a newspaper isn't tolerated in most learning events so why should instant messaging, emailing, or web browsing?)

4. For classroom learning events or longer webinars, provide just enough break time to allow time for restroom, refreshments, and quick message

Figure 3-2. Sample Letter to Trainee

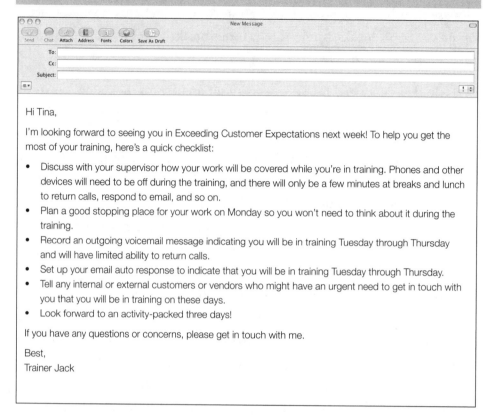

Hi Tina,

I'm looking forward to seeing you in Exceeding Customer Expectations next week! To help you get the most of your training, here's a quick checklist:

- Discuss with your supervisor how your work will be covered while you're in training. Phones and other devices will need to be off during the training, and there will only be a few minutes at breaks and lunch to return calls, respond to email, and so on.
- Plan a good stopping place for your work on Monday so you won't need to think about it during the training.
- Record an outgoing voicemail message indicating you will be in training Tuesday through Thursday and will have limited ability to return calls.
- Set up your email auto response to indicate that you will be in training Tuesday through Thursday.
- Tell any internal or external customers or vendors who might have an urgent need to get in touch with you that you will be in training on these days.
- Look forward to an activity-packed three days!

If you have any questions or concerns, please get in touch with me.

Best,
Trainer Jack

checking. Ten minutes is usually enough time to do this. Two 10-minute breaks are preferable to one 15- or 20-minute break. Consider asking participants to delay message checking until lunch or the end of the day.

5. Provide variety in the learning activities. Trainees sometimes check their phones when they are disinterested or bored. For webinars and teleclasses, use two or more speakers (male and female teams work well), use polling features frequently, and use the instant messaging feature to promote learner interaction. For teleclasses, consider using break-out groups to reduce monotony. For face-to-face classes, change activities every 20–30 minutes. Monitor body language to check for learner engagement.

6. Coaching meetings should take place in a safe and neutral environment. Meet away from the office to provide privacy and freedom from distractions.

Downside

This TIE may not be as effective as it could be if

- the culture of the organization is such that frequent interruptions are the norm
- the culture of the organization is such that people are addicted to their cell phones and personal digital assistants
- trainees are not interested in the training, or they don't understand how the learning will affect their jobs
- trainees are not held accountable for their learning or are not tested on it.

Variations

- Hold classroom training off site to reduce distractions.
- Collect phones and other devices in a basket and leave at the back of the room for retrieval as necessary and at breaks.
- Ask one person in the learning event to be the phone monitor, who can notify anyone in the class who receives an emergency call.
- Conduct shorter class sessions, increasing the number of them if necessary.
- At the beginning of the learning event, ask participants to imagine they are "on the other side of the world" or on a spaceship (choose a country or region that is not too appealing or they may start thinking about recreation), without access to the Internet, email, or voicemail. They are stranded on a desert island of learning.

Combine With

Boss Briefing/Debriefing, Apples, Target Objectives, Mind Sweep

Strategy Link: Connect Organizational Strategy to Specific Training

Who: trainer/trainee's supervisor
When: before/during/after
Media: face-to-face, e-learning, webinar, teleclass, coaching

Much has been written and discussed about the importance of strategic planning and strategy in business. Alice in Wonderland said it best: "If you don't know where you're going, you won't know when you get there." Yet participants often begin a learning event without a clue as to why they are there; what they are going to learn; why what they will learn is important to their job; and how what they will learn is linked to their organization's strategy, strategic plan, or their department goals.

Why does this happen? There are a variety of reasons. The link between senior management and the rest of the organization may not be strong, so that most employees in the organization are not aware of or cannot easily recall the organization's business strategy. The link between senior management and the learning and development function may not be strong, so that workplace learning professionals cannot incorporate the organization's business strategy into learning objectives, class activities, and learning outcomes. Often senior managers and/or workplace learning professionals assume that workers understand the link between business strategy and their own jobs, when in fact they do not. Frequently there is a vast distance between the C Suite and the front line. Even if the business strategy is known and frequently communicated, workplace learning professionals may, in sync with their traditional role, focus solely on the skills to be taught and may overlook the context of the learning, that is, how the learning supports overall business and unit goals.

These obstacles are easily overcome, assuming a strategic plan exists and is accessible, as it is in most organizations these days. When participants see a link between what they are learning and the strategy of their organization, their learning is more likely to stick.

The term strategy is used rather loosely here. One organization's strategy may be another organization's mission statement.

1. Review the organization's strategic plan. If it is not readily available, review the organization's external and internal websites for indicators and clues. For example, if the first few lines of the website say, "We have believed for decades in building quality business relationships and making recommendations that have been proven over time," this is an indicator of the business strategy. Two other examples: "We are committed to improving the quality, safety, and performance of our assets," and "We develop and build communities so people have nice places to live."

2. Review the learning objectives for a specific course or for all courses within specified areas of responsibility.

3. Determine the linkages between strategy and the skills or knowledge being taught. This may be evident or it may need to be thought through. Here are some examples:
   - If the strategy is improving quality, safety, and performance of assets, and the class is on conducting effective performance appraisals: Effective performance appraisals are linked with higher levels of employee satisfaction and better supervisor-employee communication. Higher levels of satisfaction and communication result in better quality work and support lower levels of turnover, which increases the overall quality and safety of the work. (That is, more satisfied workers are likely to do better work and conform to safety requirements and are less likely to leave the company.)
   - If the strategy is developing and building communities so people have nice places to live and the class is on effective communication skills: Project managers and line managers can save time and reduce costly errors by communicating effectively and efficiently. Reduced time on the job and rework results in better quality housing at more affordable prices.
   - If the strategy is building relationships and making recommendations that have been proven over time, and the class is on customer service, well, the link is evident here. Remember, though, that the link may

not be evident to frontline workers, and in any event, they should be reminded of it.

4. Decide how to communicate the strategy link to participants. There are several different options and many of them can be combined with other TIEs.

- The easiest option is to include a strategy link statement with the learning objectives. Either right before or immediately after the learning objectives, include a statement that links the business strategy with the learning topic, as in the examples above.

- Don't stop at repeating the strategy once. Repeat the link at various points during the learning. Good potential "strategy link points" are before and/or after skill practices, in discussions, and when introducing a new section of the learning material.

- Record a short video (two to three minutes should be long enough) of the CEO or other senior leader outlining the business strategy and the link with this learning program. Show it at the beginning of the learning. If it is only possible for the CEO to do one video segment rather than program-specific videos, show the general video and verbally make the strategy link with each course.

- Record an audio file with a message from the CEO or other senior leader, stating the strategy link. Include a link to this audio file in the pretraining registration/confirmation. Send a copy to the trainee's supervisor.

- Ask the trainee's supervisor to review the strategy link with his or her employee prior to the learning event and/or afterward.

5. When coaching, review the strategic plan at the same time that coaching outcomes are discussed and established. Consider involving the trainee's supervisor in this discussion.

6. Remember, today's employees have many things competing for their attention. Do not expect them to recall something that has been said one time. Repeat the strategy link message at various points during the learning for maximum effect.

Downside

This TIE may not be as effective as it could be if

- the organization does not have a strategy
- the strategy is considered "top secret" and is not available to nonmanagers or to external consultant trainers
- there is no connection between the organization's strategy and the learning content
- the strategy statement is so vague that it is difficult to link to the learning.

Variations

- Use departmental or work unit goals in addition to or instead of the larger organization's strategy.
- Ask participants to identify the strategy link in a class discussion.
  Take care to avoid discussing whether or not the strategy is appropriate, however.

Combine With

Boss Briefing/Debriefing, Podcasts, The Proof's in the Pudding, Target Objectives, Trainees as Teachers

Can-Do Attitude: Support Success and Positive Outcomes

Who: trainer
When: before/during/after
Media: face-to-face, e-learning, webinar, teleclass, coaching

A can-do attitude is a conviction—a belief—that whatever needs to be done, can be done and will be done. Trainees with a can-do attitude have the internal belief that they are able to take on challenges, such as learning new skills, and achieve positive outcomes. They display confidence and optimism. The formal name for this can-do attitude is called self-efficacy. Self-efficacy goes beyond an attitude of self-confidence because it is associated with several skills and behaviors that support this can-do belief. These supporting skills and behaviors are outlined in the following paragraphs.

Participants with strong self-efficacy beliefs take responsibility to make sure a job or action gets done, and they work to overcome any challenges that may stand in the way. They attribute most failures to insufficient effort. However, people with weaker self-efficacy attribute most failures to their low ability.

Closely related to taking responsibility is being accountable. High self-efficacy learners hold themselves accountable for practicing and achieving learning outcomes and for using them on the job. Low self-efficacy learners are likely to "hide" during in-class skill practices and forget about applying what they have learned once they get back to work. High self-efficacy learners are more likely to initiate a posttraining conversation with their supervisor and make an effort to practice newly learned skills once they return to work. Low self-efficacy learners are more likely to forget about applying their newly learned skills or to get caught up in daily job activities, believing they have no time for the new skills. High self-efficacy trainees not only set posttraining goals, they work diligently to achieve them. Low self-efficacy trainees may set posttraining goals, but are more easily distracted and derailed.

Attitudes and beliefs are contagious. If one or a few trainees moan, "I'll never be able to do this!" or "We don't have time to do it this way on the job," more people in the learning event, assuming they have access to one another, will begin to doubt their abilities. Group strength can also work the other way—to promote self-efficacy and learning transfer through supportive comments and encouraging behavior.

A can-do attitude originates in childhood with the messages heard at home, at school, and on the playground, as well as the experiences and successes a child encounters. These shape the child's view of the world as a supportive or unsupportive place, and whether challenges are obstacles to be overcome or confirmations of low ability.

In adults, low self-efficacy beliefs can be overcome in many ways using techniques outlined below. Workplace learning professionals can play a critical role shaping can-do beliefs for individual trainees and groups of trainees in the classroom.

Noted psychologist Albert Bandura (1997), who originated self-efficacy theory, says that people's self-efficacy beliefs can be developed through four main sources of influence, as he calls them: mastery experiences, social models (seeing people like them succeed at the task), social persuasion, and positive emotional states (moods). The steps below are based on these sources, with specific application to workplace learning and making the learning stick.

1. Review the learning objectives and identify specific, key skills to be learned. Also identify specific skills and activities that should be used on the job. There may be some variation here depending on various trainees' job titles.
2. Plan positive messages about the training content. "I know you can do it" comments are fine, but even better are comments specific to the skills being taught, such as "When you go back to work, I know and believe that you'll be able to use _____ skills without any problem." Write the comments down for easy reference during training.

3. Communicate these positive messages before the training in the course announcement and with the trainee and the trainee's supervisor.

4. Review the design of the learning. People should be placed in situations where they are likely to experience successes. Are skill practices broken down into a series of progressively difficult activities and tasks? Are there enough skill practices so that most trainees will be able to master each skill? If the course has been taught previously, were most trainees able to perform successfully? Are typical obstacles identified and discussed? Consider breaking skill practices down into smaller practices of subskills with progressive difficulty. Consider also using job aids or other methods of assistance that can be gradually withdrawn once the skill is mastered.

5. At the beginning of the learning event or beforehand, help trainees set realistic goals for their learning. Involve the trainees' supervisor if appropriate. Goals that are too lofty can undermine a can-do attitude. At the conclusion of the learning event, help trainees set realistic goals for applying and practicing the learning on the job.

6. Provide opportunities for trainees to see others like themselves using the skills. A trainee or two from a previous class could be invited back to talk about or demonstrate how they have used the skills. Fellow classmates in the same class or video clips of "real people" using the skills (digital video technology makes this very easy) will work, too.

7. Do not demonstrate the skill any more than necessary. Although a boost to the trainer's ego, demonstrations from highly skilled individuals are likely to reduce can-do beliefs in a beginner.

8. Provide pep talks throughout the learning event and afterward. Try these approaches:

   - Feel-felt-found. "You may *feel* you can't remember all these steps. Others have *felt* this way—I hear this comment often. They have *found* that once they start doing it, the steps flow easily from one to the next."

   - Personal reflection. "When I first tried this, I made so many mistakes. And I kept practicing, kept trying, and the next thing I knew, I could do it."

- Coach at halftime. "There's not one of you in here who doesn't have the brain power, the dexterity, and the physical strength to do this. You each have the ability. It's up to you to put your God-given ability to use. I know you can do it!"

Don't be afraid to show enthusiasm! Practice in front of a mirror.

1. Send pep talk messages after the learning event via email or voicemail (broadcast technology makes this a quick and easy task; see figure 3-3).

2. Shift "can't do" conversations. Throughout the classroom or coaching learning event, do not accept excuses for not being able to learn the skills or apply them to the job. Instead, shift the conversation and work with participants to develop solutions to obstacles and to accept responsibility for using them.

3. Communicate with trainees' supervisors. Ask them to shift can't-do conversations, and work with their employee to develop solutions to obstacles and to accept responsibility to use the skills.

4. Maintain a generally positive attitude throughout the learning event and afterward. Positive mental states (moods) encourage higher levels of participant self-efficacy. Avoid complaining about the training room, refreshments, or other logistics. Read a book or listen to a recording on positive mental attitude to help you prepare to do this. To foster participants' positive moods, the trainer must have one as well. A generally positive attitude helps learners develop and maintain self-efficacy beliefs.

Figure 3-3. Sample Pep Talk Message

**Practicing good safety is a snap...
you'll get the hang of it!**

Downside

This TIE may not be as effective as it could be if

- there is too much learning content to be covered in the time/space available and not enough time for practice
- generally negative, unsupportive attitudes pervade the workplace organization and the training room
- the trainer's ego is such that he or she prefers to demonstrate his or her own skills rather than assist trainees in developing theirs
- a general practice of blaming and finger pointing works against trainees accepting responsibility for learning and using skills.

Variations

- Invite previous participants to deliver the pep talk. Consider coaching them to be sure they deliver the intended message, with enthusiasm.
- Shoot a short video clip of a previous participant performing the skill and include it in precourse announcements and in the course introduction.
- Shoot a short video clip of a previous participant talking about using the skill and how it has helped him or her do the job better.
- Keep a camcorder handy in the classroom or coaching session and shoot short clips of participants performing the skill. Play some of these in later classes. (The video file can easily be inserted into the presentation graphics.)
- In the learning event or afterward, provide a list of how previous participants successfully overcame obstacles.
- Hold a specific discussion on whether the participants are willing to engage in a learning process. Discuss what it means to participate in the learning experience, especially if it is an ongoing continuous coaching type of process. Clarify the joint responsibility of trainer/coach and trainee/coachee to partner for results.

Combine With

Boss Briefing/Debriefing, Podcasts, Apples, Trainees as Teachers, Screen Saver

The Proof's in the Pudding: Use Testimonials to Build Support and Positive Expectations

Who: trainer
When: before
Media: face-to-face, e-learning, webinar, teleclass, coaching

Making a major purchase—one that involves a good deal of money or time (a vacation, for example)—generally requires careful thought and planning. Making a major commitment for a learning event that involves some or a lot of time and energy also requires careful thought and planning for most people. Before buying a car, for example, most people read reviews and consumer information, and they talk to friends, colleagues, or even perfect strangers about how satisfactory their experience has been.

Why should learning be any different? Although the learning may be mandatory and in most cases the funding doesn't come from a participant's own pocket, learning about other people's experiences builds commitment for the decision to attend and the motivation to learn and apply the learning. Increased commitment and motivation result in higher levels of training transfer.

Often talking with peers who have attended the training helps participants gain a better understanding about the content and expected outcomes than reading the course description or even talking with their supervisor about it. Specific feedback from previous attendees helps new participants not only understand the content and how they will be able to apply it to their jobs, but such information also helps them build positive expectations for their learning experience. Positive expectations make positive results more likely.

Sometimes past and future participants are acquainted with each other and can easily share feedback. Other times workplace learning professionals play a key role in helping to connect previous participants with future ones. If opportunities for casual, informal information sharing are limited, or if the workplace learning professional does not know if opportunities for this exist, more structured approaches are helpful.

Testimonials in the course descriptions and in registration confirmation materials provide another way to help participants gain an understanding of previous participants' experiences.

Remember the goal is to set the psychological stage for a positive learning experience and for practical expectations as to how the learning content will be applied later.

After the learning event, feedback and networking with others who have participated is also helpful. Discussing and sharing how they have used the learning is addressed in the TIE Success Stories and Lessons Learned.

1. Review end-of-session evaluations for comments and feedback. This information is usually gathered for other purposes, so it should be readily available for this purpose as well.

2. Capture the comments. Although positive feedback is most helpful, other comments will provide balanced feedback and may be helpful as well. Specific comments are better than more general comments. For example, "Good session, I learned a lot" can be used, but "Learning how to use a safety harness the right way was a real eye-opener. I'll never do it the wrong way again" is even more helpful feedback to provide to future participants.

3. Capture end-of-session evaluation metrics as well. Summarize them with statements such as, "75 percent of previous participants rated this class excellent or superior."

4. Solicit additional comments from previous participants and their managers on how they are using what they have learned. Again, specific comments are preferred.

5. Include these comments and metrics in the course description for future participants (see figure 3-4) and in the registration confirmation that is sent once they are enrolled.

6. Include in the registration confirmation the names of previous participants in the same department, division, or work unit. This information is usually readily available in most learning management systems. Encourage the new participant to talk with previous participants about how they are using what they have learned.

Figure 3-4. Course Description Example

Managing Multiple Priorities

Appropriate for All Levels

We all have the same 24 hours, but how we manage this time can make a big difference in work effectiveness. This interactive course explores key strengths and areas to improve for each participant in 12 key areas. Detailed action plans are included to maximize after-workshop practice.

> *I can get a lot more done now after taking this class. I learned techniques for how to follow my action plan and track my progress. I highly recommend this class for anyone who wants to get more done in less time.* —Paul Participant

Workshop Content

The following is a sampling of what may be covered in the workshop, depending on specific needs and Time Mastery Profile results. Methods used include video/DVD, didactic information, Socratic questioning, small group discussion, and individual activities.

I. Introduction: the importance and uniqueness of time as a resource

    a. We each have the same 24 hours.
    b. It's not possible to save time and bank it or to borrow it.
    c. Demonstration: how effective time management can increase effective time use.
    d. Etc.

---

7. For coaching, guard against using coaching solely for poor performers and corrective action. Link individuals who have experienced positive, rapid, proactive learning through coaching with individuals who may be considering it or who have been referred for coaching.

Downside

This TIE may not be as effective as it could be if

- previous participants have not had a positive learning experience (it may be time for a redesign)
- previous participants have not commented on how they will use what they have learned (Do they know? Additional investigation may be required.)
- course descriptions and confirmation of learner registrations do not include fields for these testimonials
- previous participants do not want to share their experience with new participants (What is wrong with this work culture?).

Variations

- Ask new participants' managers to tell them who in the department has previously attended the training and encourage them to talk to each other.
- Invite a few previous learners to participate in the first segments of the learning event, to share their experience with how they are using the learning.
- Record a short focus group of previous participants, discussing what they have learned and how they use it. Include short clips of these video or audio testimonials in the course description and registration confirmation.
- Post testimonials on a centrally located bulletin board, by a frequently used copier or printer, or by the elevators.
- Post testimonials on an electronic bulletin board on the learning and development website.
- Designate a table in the cafeteria on a specific day(s) as Name of the Course Table and invite previous and registered participants to sit together. If the budget allows, pay for the lunch of people who participate. A facilitator is not required, but is probably a good idea.
- Put testimonials on a coffee mug or other piece of marketing collateral.

Combine With

Boss Briefing/Debriefing, Podcasts, Can-Do Attitude, Trainees as Teachers

Seeds: Plant Extroverts to Germinate Application Participation

Who: trainer
When: before/during
Media: face-to-face, webinar, teleclass

Training events with active, verbal participants tend to result in higher training transfer than events where participants are quiet and reserved. Classes heavily populated with extroverts or classes with equal numbers of introverts and extroverts have more verbalization of ideas, concepts, and learnings. Lower levels of verbalization tend to result in lower levels of transfer. This is true whether the learning content is of a technical nature, soft skills, or compliance types of training, such as ethics. "Seeding" classes, small group activities, and field practice with more verbal participants will help increase the learning for participants who are more reserved or quiet.

Most trainers who have had an entire class of quiet and reserved participants would agree that this type of class is more difficult to work with. The trainees do sit attentively during instructor-led portions of the learning, true, but the instructor gets little feedback as to how much of the content is being understood. There are fewer questions, less interaction, less positive attitudes toward future implementation, and less engaged skill practice. Unless the instructor has a thorough understanding of the trainees' job titles, the link between learning and application may be lost.

This is not to say that introverts are not good students or that being a reflective type of learner is bad. It is just that when it comes to training classes, research shows that the learning is more likely to be transferred to the job when some extroverts are present.

Most classes do have at least a few individuals who ask questions and make comments, fortunately. Having a class full of extroverts can also present its own challenges with keeping them focused and on task.

How much influence does a trainer have as to who is in the class? Some workplace learning professionals are familiar with participants and are able to review class lists to make some adjustments as to which participants are in which class sections. Other instructors must make do with whomever shows up. All trainers, however, are able to influence how they handle participants once they are in the learning event.

1. Check class lists in advance of the training event. If some or all participants are known, identify the quiet and reflective learners and the more active and outgoing learners.

2. If the trainees are not known, ask supervisors, other trainers who may have had them in class, or others who will know how active a participant tends to be in the classroom.

3. It isn't necessary to do the above for the entire training class. Simply identify enough participants to be certain at least a few active and outgoing participants will be in the class.

4. If necessary and if there are multiple sections of the class, redistribute the learners to achieve some balance.

5. At the beginning and throughout the learning event, monitor and encourage some level of participation and verbalization. Here are a few suggestions for doing this:

    • Use an icebreaker that requires participants to interact with one another. Just two to three minutes of talking with two to four fellow participants will lead to higher levels of participation and discussion throughout the class. Going around the room with each participant giving their name and so forth should be avoided because this activity does not "break the ice" and help participants open up.

    • Ask open-ended questions of the group as a whole, such as, "What do you think the biggest challenge is in using the process we're going to learn?" "How will the skills we are going to learn here help you do your job better?" The purpose is to get the ball rolling, to encourage people to talk, and to observe how verbal the group is.

6. Observe participants during the icebreaker and during the first minutes or hours of the training. Who is more active and outgoing? Who is more

reserved and reflective? Be on the lookout for individuals who may appear interested but do not participate in class discussions, do not ask questions, and in general seem reluctant to verbalize.

7. Mix the group so that the active participants are interspersed with the reflective ones. For small group activities and practice in the field, "seed" extroverts in with more reserved participants.

8. Provide time for writing down responses before discussion. In this way, introverted learners have time to reflect, and then everyone can learn from the subsequent discussion.

Downside

This TIE may not be as effective as it could be if

- the instructor does not assess the trainee characteristics and adjust accordingly
- the trainer is more concerned with delivering information than with being sure that learning takes place
- the learning design does not allow time for discussion, interaction, and questions
- management does not provide the necessary trainee information when requested
- there is a prevailing belief that all participants should be treated equally, and that trainee characteristics should not be acknowledged.

Combine With

Boss Briefing/Debriefing, Can-Do Attitude, Apples, Color in the Classroom, Training Buddies

Apples: Minimize the Influence of Some Participants

Who: trainer
When: before/during
Media: face-to-face, webinar, teleclass

There is an old saying: "one bad apple spoils the barrel." When learners interact, they influence one another. Learners without attitudes and other characteristics that support training transfer are less likely to make the training stick.

Any trainer who has had an entire class of complainers or trainees with low levels of motivation can attest to how different the learning experience is under these circumstances. Trainees ask few if any questions. Nonverbals signal their attitudes and lack of receptivity: slouched posture, bored facial expressions, expressionless tones of voice, using their phone or other electronic device, and even reading the paper during class. They may try to engage other trainees in side conversations. They participate in activities and other aspects of the learning event just enough to get by.

Fortunately a learning event is not often filled with these bad apples. But frequently there are one or a few of them, and they can spoil the whole class if a trainer isn't careful.

A recent survey of workplace learning professionals indicated that trainers tend to underestimate the importance of trainee characteristics and the role these play in training transfer. Specifically, the following trainee characteristics, among others mentioned in the section on background and research, have been found to result in lower levels of training transfer:

- **Negative attitude.** Trainees with an overall negative attitude (the formal term is *affect*) and low motivation to learn tend to have lower levels of training transfer.
- **Low achievement motivation.** Trainees with little interest in advancing their careers or doing their jobs better tend to show lower levels of training transfer.

How much influence does a trainer have as to who is in the class? Some workplace learning professionals are able to review class lists and make some adjustments as to which participants are in which class sections. Other instructors must make do with whomever shows up. All trainers, however, are able to influence how they handle participants with the above characteristics once they are in the learning event.

1. Identify those who have registered for training as far in advance as possible. Class lists are usually accessible through electronic registration systems or a training coordinator if the trainer does not handle registration personally.
2. If the trainer knows some or all of the trainees, identify those individuals whose attitudes and motivation may limit class learning.
3. If the trainees are not known, ask supervisors, other trainers who may have had them in class, or others who will know if there is anyone registered who may have a negative attitude or low motivation to learn.
4. If multiple sections of the class are being offered, distribute the individuals with the limiting characteristics throughout the sections, having as few as possible in a single section. If the class is offered in an alternative format, such as e-learning, encourage their enrollment in this format.
5. At the beginning and throughout the learning event, identify participants who display negative attitudes and low motivation. Their nonverbals will identify them: slouched posture, bored facial expressions, using their phone or other electronic devices, reading the paper during class, rolling their eyes, engaging in side conversations. Comments such as "I'm just here for the donuts," "This will never work," and "I'm just here because I was told I had to come" are also key identifiers.
6. Identify through informal conversation or comments made in class any bad apples who may be quite skilled and feel they should not have to attend the training. Recognize their skill by asking them for examples and having them assist in demonstrations. Recognizing their skills or experience can often turn around their attitude.
7. Reposition seating so these individuals are in the front of the classroom. Often a private conversation will dispel some of the negative attitude and

low motivation. A simple, discrete request to turn off the phone or put away the newspaper sends the message that their behavior is not acceptable and often is enough to get them to stop.

8. If the behavior continues, put these individuals in small groups or practice sessions together so they are not mixed in with other participants. Don't let a bad apple spoil the training for the rest of the trainees.

9. Don't ignore these individuals with negative attitudes and low motivation. Address negative comments made in class by saying, "I understand this is your opinion. Others feel differently." Then move on with the discussion.

10. For coaching and other one-on-one work, hold a targeted discussion as to whether the participant is willing to engage in this learning process. In some cases, it may be necessary to hold more than one of these discussions if the participant's nonverbals tend to signal unwillingness or disinterest. Emphasize the joint responsibility between coach and participant for the outcomes.

Downside

This TIE may not be as effective as it could be if

-   class lists are not accessible in advance
-   participants are not known to the trainer and it isn't possible to obtain advance information about them
-   the trainer is not sensitive to nonverbal and verbal indications of negative attitude and low motivation
-   management does not provide the necessary trainee background information when requested
-   there is a prevailing belief that all participants should be treated equally and that negative attitudes and low motivation should not be acknowledged.

Variations

-   Assign participants identified as possibly having negative attitudes or low motivation to the same class section. The reasoning here is that if they are contained in a single class they will not contaminate other participants and other classes.

- Assign bad apples to different small groups or practice teams. Ask the other participants in these groups to assist these individuals.

Combine With

Boss Briefing/Debriefing, Seeds, Training Buddies

Target Objectives: Involve, Personalize, Engage

Who: trainer/trainee
When: before/during
Media: face-to-face, e-learning, webinar, teleclass,
coaching

Training objectives are an important part of almost every training program and learning event. The format of the objective may vary. Some instructional designers and trainers prefer to use objectives that are stated in general terms such as "understand how to conduct performance appraisals." Others prefer to use objectives that include a condition, the performance, and measurable criteria such as "given a performance review form, the participant will demonstrate a successful performance appraisal discussion using the three key points and four critical behaviors identified in the class."

Regardless of the format used, objectives are an important aspect of each learning event because they indicate the content for the learning event— what is most important and what the participants can expect to learn. Training objectives are one-way communications from the trainer/instructional designer/coach to the participant.

But what about the learner? Often learners are interested in some of the learning objectives and not others. Or some of the learning objectives and the learning content have a higher priority than others for some learners or are more applicable to certain job titles. This information may be informally communicated to the trainer at the beginning of the learning event, but by then it is usually too late to make major adjustments in the learning content.

Instead, ask participants and perhaps their managers ahead of time which course objectives are most important to them for their job (see figure 3-5). Doing this has several advantages. First, it provides a pretraining opportunity for two-way communication between trainer and trainee, which is usually helpful. Second, the trainer receives valuable information at a time when he or she can be most responsive—before the learning event, when there is time to adjust if

Figure 3-5. Personal Learning Objectives

 You will be attending the workshop Leadership Skills soon. To help you get the most out of this class, please read over the objectives from the list below and check the ones that are most important to you. In the blanks, write how you will be able to use the objective to help you do your job better. Also add anything you want to learn that is not listed. We'll do our best to accommodate you.

☐ Understand your leadership/management style—strengths and areas to improve

_____

☐ Learn how to respond to employees differently based on their style

_____

☐ Learn how to choose the best response for almost any situation

_____

☐ Learn how to motivate people to get the best results

_____

☐ Learn how to coach people to better performance

_____

☐ _____

☐ _____

Now Focus on Your Own Objectives/Outcomes

Keeping the above objectives/outcomes in mind, what additional objectives/outcomes do you want to achieve from this training program?

Objectives

1. _____
2. _____
3. _____

Please go over your objectives with your manager and bring this sheet with you to the first session.

necessary. Third, by introducing the course information to the learners or reminding them of it, the trainer has an opportunity to set positive expectations for the learning. Finally, reviewing and prioritizing the objectives may cause learners to talk with others—peers, their manager—about the learning.

If it is not possible to ask participants to prioritize objectives ahead of time, it is still helpful to ask them to prioritize the objectives at the beginning of the learning event. Even though the learning design can't be altered significantly, more time could be devoted to higher priority objectives. In an e-learning format, a prioritizing activity could be included at the beginning with guidance to place the most focus and time on the higher-priority modules.

If it is impossible to make any adjustments in the content, such as in compliance training or an e-learning format, targeting objectives may be still be helpful. Participants could be asked to test out or skip certain sections that are not relevant or necessary.

1. Review the objectives for the learning event and determine whether to use a general format or a more specific format (see above). Even though the more specific format may be used in the learning event itself, this format may be a bit clumsy for Target Objectives.

2. Communicate with participants, asking each of them to prioritize the objectives that are most important for their job. Include a "back by" deadline or ask them to bring their prioritized objectives with them. Using a special form or format may increase visibility and increase response rate.

3. Consider asking participants to add additional learning objectives or learning needs. Doing this may create more problems than it solves, but if this is the first time or two that a learning event is being conducted, it may be a good idea.

4. For coaching or other one-on-one learning, ask the participant to bring a list of specific outcomes he or she wants from coaching. This is important even if there are designated outcomes provided by the coachee's supervisor. Blend the objectives of both for best coaching results.

5. Be sure to be responsive to the prioritized objectives provided. It may be challenging if the priorities from various participants are quite different. It may be necessary to stick with the original program without adjustments, but be sure to acknowledge receiving the objectives and share with participants at the beginning of the program how the learning content was or was not adjusted and why.

6. Remember that whether or not the content has been adjusted, the other purposes of this activity will still have been met. Participants will have engaged with the learning material prior to the event, setting positive expectations and getting motivated to learn. They may also be prompted to talk with their manager and perhaps some peers who have previously attended about how the learning can be applied to the job.

Downside

This TIE may not be as effective as it could be if

- the objectives are not clearly stated
- the objectives do not accurately represent the learning content covered in the course
- participants do not respond to the request to prioritize objectives
- participants add learning objectives to their list that cannot be included in the learning event (Is this learning really relevant for their job? Do they belong in this training?)
- the trainer is unresponsive to the prioritized objectives provided
- the learning content is sequential and does not lend itself to change.

Variations

- Ask trainees' managers, rather than the trainees, to prioritize the objectives.
- Ask previous participants to prioritize which objectives were most helpful to them, and share this information with participants in upcoming learning events.
- Begin the learning event with an objective-prioritizing activity.
- At the conclusion of the class, ask participants to prioritize which objectives will be most important for them as they take their learning back to their job.

Combine With

Boss Briefing/Debriefing, Strategy Link, The Proof's in the Pudding, Use It or Lose It Checklist, Training Buddies

Color in the Classroom: Support Your Content a Different Way

Who: trainer
When: before/during
Media: face-to-face, e-learning, webinar

When you think about the color red, what comes to mind? What about green? If you are like most people, the color red tends to elicit impressions of action, heat, and intensity, whereas the color green makes one think of cool, reserve, and reflection.

Light striking the eye sets up reactions that spread throughout an organism. These responses include excitation, depression, quickened nervous response, or tranquility. Although some of our associations with colors are related to past personal experiences, researchers in the field of color psychology have found many associations with certain colors that are common to most individuals. These associations can be used to support learning objectives and thus increase retention and transfer of the learning to the job.

One experiment measured muscle responses under colored lights. Under red lights, responses were 12 percent quicker than under neutral lights (Birren, 1961). Responses under green lights were 5 percent slower. In other research, red has been found to enhance performance in athletic and other types of competitions (Hill and Barton, 2005).

Faber Birren (1961), well-known color researcher, tells us that red is generally considered to be inciting to activity and favorable for emotionally determined actions. It tends to produce the "emotional background" from which ideas and actions come forth. Green tends to create a reflection and thoughtfulness and exact fulfillment of a task and tends to produce the emotional background from which ideas are developed and actions are executed. Yellow tends to create a climate of receptivity, suggestability, and openness to outside influences. Blue tends to create a climate of reserve, passivity, and tendency to preserve the status quo. (Ever see a fast food restaurant décor in blues and greens?)

Although there are artistic considerations as well, using certain colors to support specific learning objectives will evoke a complementary emotional response. When cognitive learning is supported with emotion, it seems reasonable that the learning will be retained better and therefore more likely to stick.

Table 3-1 provides some guidance for designing virtual classrooms as well as visual aids including slides and flip chart marker colors in the face-to-face classroom.

A word about color blindness: Because color blindness is a sex-linked characteristic (it is a recessive characteristic carried on the X chromosome), 5 percent

Table 3-1. Possible Color Combinations for the Classroom and Virtual Classroom

Color	Mental Associations	Use to Support These Messages
Red	Fire, hot, emergency, blood	Action, forceful, heat, speed, emergency
Yellow	Sun, caution	Cheer, inspiration, vital, warning
Orange (Red + Yellow)	Warmth, autumn, glowing	Lively, energetic, forceful, exuberance
Blue	Sky, water, cold, sadness	Subdued, sober, reflective, passivity, quiet, melancholy
Green (Yellow + Blue)	Nature, money	Refreshing, peaceful, nascent, quiet, wealth, exact attention to detail
Purple (Red + Blue)	Royalty, height, spirituality	Dignity, lofty
Black	Death, night, the dark side, evil	(As background, not font) Disadvantages, downside, dull, bad
White	Goodness, light, purity	Advantages, pluses, brightness, good

of men are color blind and 0.5 percent of women are color blind. The most common form of color blindness is red-green, where these colors are seen as gray with no distinction between them. Yellow is usually seen as either white or brown. So the emotional effects of red, green, and in some cases yellow and blue may be lost on a very small percentage of men (and an infinitesimal number of women). When designing virtual classrooms and visuals for face-to-face classrooms, avoid red-green contrasts (red on green background or vice versa). Yellow on red or green background is usually OK because yellow is lighter, will be seen as white or brown, and can be distinguished from a background of any color.

1. Select a class and determine whether it is action or skill focused or whether it is focused on building knowledge. Is the nature of the class "get out there and do it" or is it reflective? Review the objectives to help make this determination. It is possible that some parts of the class may be action oriented and other parts reflective.

2. Choose a color or color scheme that supports this theme. For action- or skill-focused learning, use shades of red or yellow. For knowledge or reflective learning, use shades of blue or green. If a particular color is associated with the course subject matter, this may be used as well. For example, a class that provides information about finance or making money might have blue as the predominant color (knowledge), with green as an accent color (money), and splashes of red (action) throughout.

3. Consult the design templates available for the virtual classroom authoring and for slide graphics in the face-to-face classroom. The color schemes of most design templates often can be changed without changing other design features.

4. Once the overall color scheme has been chosen, support particular modules, sections, or specific views with appropriate colors in backgrounds, fonts, and/or graphics.

5. In the face-to-face classroom, choose flip chart marker colors that support your messages or themes.

Downside

This TIE may not be as effective as it could be if

- Other associations with particular colors—company culture symbols or past personal experiences—clash with or override the intended association.
- Templates from software may not provide the desired color combinations or color emphasis. (Hint: Many design templates can be overridden while preserving the basic design scheme. Look for menu items such as "color scheme.")
- Too many colors are used, resulting in a visual hodgepodge that is not pleasing to the eye and detracts from rather than supports the learning objectives. Show drafts and get feedback from someone with a "good eye," that is, a good visual sense.

Variations

- In addition to or instead of changing the color scheme of the virtual classroom or of visuals in the face-to-face classroom, add occasional, peripheral, casual color splashes, such as photos, clip art, tablecloths, break table wear, and decorative items.
- Use supportive color schemes in handouts and other participant materials. Reproduce black-and-white handouts on colored paper, using different colors for different parts of the training. Use colored clip art, photos, and other color splashes on handouts that will be printed in color. When choosing the colored items, keep in mind which colors you would like to dominate the page to support your learning objective.

Combine With

Target Objectives, Credit Cards, Use It or Lose It Checklist, Screen Saver, Webpage

Credit Cards: Reward Success in Tangible and Spendable Ways

Who: trainer/trainee's supervisor
When: after
Media: face-to-face, e-learning, webinar, teleclass, coaching

One of the most effective, and most researched, methods for changing human behavior (and animal behavior too, for that matter) is reinforcement. As behaviorist psychologists discovered, when a particular behavior is rewarded it is likely to be repeated. They also found that when a particular behavior is punished it is less likely to be repeated and that positive reinforcement is more likely than punishment to produce the desired behavior changes.

Credit cards are a way to reinforce the use of skills learned (that is, desired behaviors) when they occur on the job. They are given to trainees when they successfully use—or try to use—skills learned in training.

Different options are available to choose from: pre-loaded gift cards, fake paper cards good for credit at the company cafeteria or company store, or credit in the company's incentive gift program. The monetary value of the card is less important than the message it sends, which is to reward the desired behavior.

The trainee's supervisor is typically the one who will be able to observe the on-the-job performance to be rewarded, and it may make sense for him or her to hand out the credit cards as appropriate. The trainer may also want to maintain some connection to help the supervisor remember to use the cards as intended. Peers or others who may see the participant's performance might also be enlisted to give out a credit card.

Regardless of who will give out credit cards, it will probably be easier for the cards to be part of the particular learning event budget. The cards are then a part of the learning event and can be distributed to supervisors afterward, with instructions and reminders as to the specific performances to reward.

1. Identify which skills or behaviors should be reinforced. Review the training objectives. Consult with supervisors or other individuals who may be helpful in pinpointing which behaviors or skills are most important and are going to be used most often on the job. Make a list of these on-the-job skills or behaviors. Use different versions of this list for different job titles.

2. Determine how to document or verify that the desired behaviors are being used on the job. Possibilities include an electronic or hard copy supervisor sign-off or peer sign-off, or a fill-in-the-blank form for the participant to describe what he or she did using the skill or behavior on the job.

3. Choose a time period or time periods to check on performance. The best after-training point in time will depend on whether the goal of the credit card is to encourage participants to practice new skills immediately after training, or if the goal is to use the new skills on an ongoing basis—or both. Popular time periods are three days following training, six weeks following training, three months following training, nine months following training, and one year following training. The more check-in times, the more potential there is to award credit cards. The more credit cards awarded, the more likely learners will use the targeted skills or behaviors on an ongoing basis.

4. Purchase gift cards or pre-loaded credit cards. Most people appreciate a card that can be used in many different stores such as a pre-loaded major credit card. Link the amounts of the cards with skills to be demonstrated. Award higher denomination cards for more difficult skills. Some stores may donate small denomination gift cards if you ask, especially if it is a nonprofit or public sector organization. (Be cautious with using gift cards more than $25 or so, though, as they may be considered taxable income. Check with the appropriate department in your organization for guidance.)

5. During training, introduce the targeted list of behaviors. This can be done all at once and as they occur in the learning event. Maximize the effect of the announcement(s) with visuals of the credit cards and the list of targeted

behaviors. Link the word "credit" with the goal here (for example, "get credit for using these new skills"). At various points in the training, remind participants of the promised rewards. Provide the documentation forms in training or wait until later.

6. At the established time interval(s), send the documentation form to all trainees and their supervisors with a list of the targeted skills or behaviors and a note reminding them of the credit card reward.

7. Send or deliver credit cards as soon as possible after receipt of the documentation or deliver them to trainees' supervisors after training so that the supervisor can deliver them when the time comes. Clarify and confirm that the reason the participant is receiving the card is because he or she used the appropriate specific behavior or skill.

Downside

This TIE may not be as effective as it could be if

- Credit cards are distributed for behaviors not appearing on the predetermined list, or they are distributed in other ways to other people. For best effect, these cards should be given out only for use of the targeted behaviors or skills.
- Participants or supervisors don't report use of targeted behaviors.
- The workplace learning professional or supervisor does not deliver the reward immediately after receiving documentation of skill use.
- The credit cards are not valued by participants. This may happen if the amount of the cards is considered to be "not worth the trouble."

Variations

- Provide internally created credit cards for various tangible or intangible items, such as a day or a few hours off, logo shirt, lunch with the president, and so on. Some items may be unconventional, but be sure that most items will be appealing to most participants.
- Post facsimiles of credit cards with trainees' names on them on a bulletin board so all can see. Be sure to indicate someplace on the bulletin board which skills or behaviors they have demonstrated in their job.

- Do not give credit cards to all trainees who use skills learned in training. Place the names of those who do in a drawing, and the winner of the drawing receives a card.
- Do not attach a value to the credit card. Use them in the same way but their value will be symbolic, not monetary.

Combine With

Boss Briefing/Debriefing, Target Objectives, Success Stories and Lessons Learned, Use It or Lose It Checklist, Training Buddies

Trainees as Teachers: Give Participants a Turn to Teach and Engage

Who: trainee
When: during/after
Media: face-to-face, webinar, teleclass

People often say the best way to learn something well is to teach it. Participants often give the highest evaluation scores to their instructor when they have participated heavily in the learning event (ironically). Put these two together, and it makes sense to have trainees participate in the facilitation of the class.

Trainees of course are not subject matter experts (SMEs); otherwise they would not be trainees. It is not necessary, however, to be a SME to present a small piece of learning material or to facilitate a discussion. In fact, sometimes participants feel that non-SME trainers are more approachable, more "real," more like themselves. Non-SME trainers also may be able to "get down to the level" of the trainee and provide explanations that are more understandable than what a SME provides. Participants may be more likely to ask questions and perhaps to show their ignorance of a particular skill or concept with a non-SME trainer.

Teaching or facilitating an entire class probably does not make sense, of course. Assigning trainees to lead small sections of learning content, however, has many advantages, particularly for classes that last many days or weeks:

- It provides an opportunity for the learners to review or study the material in more depth than they otherwise might do.
- It provides active learner involvement.
- It provides feedback to the trainer as to how well class material is being learned.

A side benefit of enlisting trainees to facilitate parts of the class is that the trainer has an opportunity to sit down and take a few minutes out of the spotlight.

1. Review the course design and determine small chunks of content that could be assigned to trainees to teach. Choose content that is relatively

easy and that does not require mastery of previous skills or concepts. Decide how many content chunks to "delegate." Will all trainees facilitate a chunk or just a few trainees?

2. If only a few trainees will be teaching, how will they be identified? Volunteer? Assign? Random, such as drawing straws? Many participants will be hesitant to volunteer for such an assignment so it is a good idea to have a back-up plan even if the first plan is to call for volunteers.

3. Decide how to involve trainees. These are some options:

   • Have the trainee present a small portion of lecture content to the entire class.

   • Have trainees present small portions of lecture content concurrently to another trainee or small group of trainees. This approach reduces the stage fright that so often accompanies speaking to a larger audience and provides more trainees with the opportunity to present. Although a bit more complicated, this approach can also be used in a webinar or teleclass by having separate chat or phone lines.

   • Ask the trainee to demonstrate the application of a chunk of learning content. For example, the instructor gives a lesson on how to perform a particular procedure, and the trainee demonstrates it.

   • Have the trainee facilitate a class discussion of a particular concept or skill. The instructor may want to provide some questions to the trainee/teacher.

   • Ask the trainee to facilitate a concurrent small group discussion of a particular concept or skill. As with presenting to a small group, this approach reduces stage fright and provides more trainees with the opportunity to facilitate.

4. Determine whether any additional space or different room setup will be needed. Most trainees are comfortable with concurrent break-out groups, but if the room is small or the table/chair configuration does not lend itself to break-out groups, another room close by may be a better option. Space that may work for short concurrent leaderless discussion groups may not work as well when trainees are teaching or facilitating.

5. At the beginning of the class, mention that participants will be leading some of the learning. Demonstrate confidence and optimism in the train- ees' ability to do this, and point out that by teaching they are better able to learn.

6. During and after each participant presentation, demonstration, or facili- tation, lead applause or other demonstrations of appreciation. Avoid the temptation to correct or interrupt unless absolutely necessary. If it is neces- sary to correct, try to do so after rather than during.

7. For coaching and other one-on-one learning, encourage the coachee to take on an action learning project where he or she teaches or shows some- one a new skill (such as facilitating a meeting, planning a project, and so on). Observe and provide feedback.

Downside

This TIE may not be as effective as it could be if

- the learning content is extremely complex or does not lend itself to being broken up into chunks
- trainees lack self-confidence and the belief that they can help others learn
- the instructor has difficulty seeing someone present, demonstrate, or facili- tate in a less-than-perfect fashion
- the participants are resistant to participative learning and would rather sit back and be taught.

Variations

- Trainees could present a separate session after the learning event, such as a brown bag lunch session.
- Previous participants could provide a brief presentation, summary, or content chunk as part of a staff meeting in their department.
- Trainees could present, demonstrate, or facilitate a content chunk for a later training class.
- Before the workshop, assign trainees the content they will deliver so they can be mentally prepared.

- Trainees could use open source electronic technology (wiki) to share knowledge or facilitate a content chunk before or after the learning event—or in the midst of an e-learning course. In this case all trainees participate in guiding each others' learning in a collaborative environment. It may be helpful, though, to designate one participant as a lead.

Combine With

Can-Do Attitude, Seeds, Sticky Sessions, Webpage

Success Stories and Lessons Learned: Encourage Participants to Share

Who: trainee
When: after
Media: face-to-face, e-learning, webinar, teleclass, coaching

When participants return to work after a learning event, it is hoped they will try out the skills they learned. They may do this on their own or with the help of their supervisor or a peer. Sometimes trainees successfully perform the skill on the first or second try, but sometimes they run into problems or obstacles. They may not be able to recall a crucial step in a process, or what felt right when tried in the training room seems awkward later. This is a critical point in all trainees' learning and unfortunately they often face it alone. Unless they work in the same department or work area, trainees seldom see or interact with one another after a learning event.

If trainees can determine what they are doing wrong and correct it, they will continue using the skills. However, if they are not aware that they are doing something incorrectly, if they are not able to determine what they are doing wrong, or if they aren't able to make corrections, they will perform the skills incorrectly for a long time, maybe years.

The trainee may ask his or her supervisor for assistance or feedback, but the supervisor may or may not know how to perform the new skills correctly. Even if the supervisor previously used the skill, procedures may have changed. The trainee may ask a fellow employee, but this person may or may not know the right way to do it. Even if the trainee is performing the new skills correctly, he or she may want or need feedback to be sure.

Trainees need a forum, an opportunity to communicate with classmates and others who have recently completed the training to discuss hurdles they encounter, to get feedback and assistance, and to share successes. The forum also can provide a safe place to ask questions without feeling stupid in front of their supervisor or peers.

The forum can take many forms. Trainees may form a support group that meets for a few times after training, either in person or virtually. The training may include a follow-up session facilitated by the trainer to address issues that come up when trying out the new skills. Or the forum may be an open, two-way communication vehicle, such as a virtual discussion group or bulletin board (see figure 3-6), so that trainees can get assistance from the trainer and from each other with using the skills taught in training. Equally important, the forum can be an opportunity to share and celebrate each others' successes.

1. Review the learning objectives for the course and identify the skills trainees are expected to use soon after returning from training. If necessary, shorten this list by identifying which skills they are more likely to have trouble with and/or the skills for which they are least likely to have help and support on the job. Are the skills complex but used often, so that once the trainees learn them, they are likely to remember them? Or, will the skills be used less frequently so that trainees may need a resource at the time they need to use them?

2. Reflect on the target population, that is, the typical trainees who attend this training. Are they geographically dispersed, or are many of them in the same location? Do they use the computer regularly and easily? What is their role and level within the organization? Do they operate independently or are they closely supervised on the job?

3. Identify potential resources and options for a post-training forum. These include
   - An electronic bulletin board or discussion group where trainees can post issues, concerns, and successes, and where others can post suggestions, advice, and "attaboys" or "attagirls". Most email software can set up discussion groups, or these could be accessed from the organization's intranet or the learning and development department website.
   - A special table in the cafeteria for class graduates to sit and share on a specific day or on a regular basis.
   - A teleconference or series of teleconferences. Find out whether or not your organization uses a teleconferencing service. If not, free services are easily located.

Figure 3-6. Support Group Discussion Board Posts

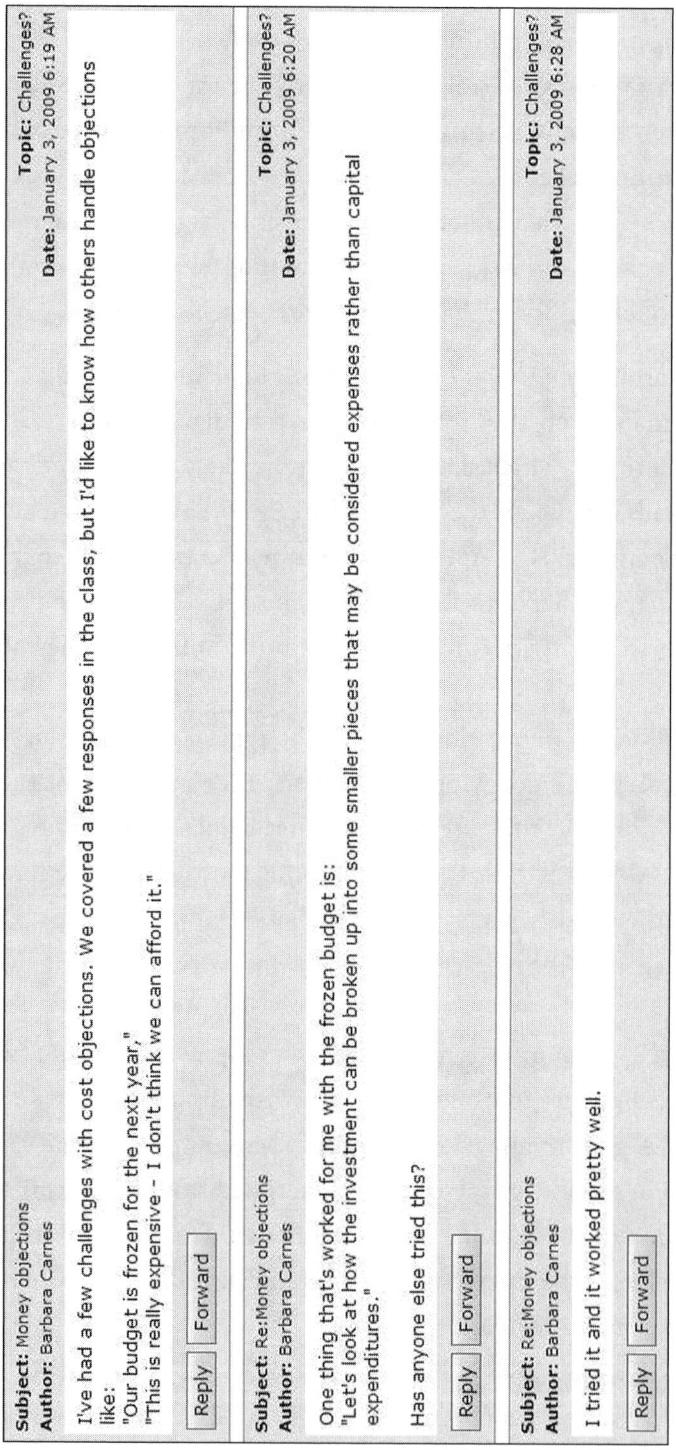

Subject: Money objections
Author: Barbara Carnes

Topic: Challenges?
Date: January 3, 2009 6:19 AM

I've had a few challenges with cost objections. We covered a few responses in the class, but I'd like to know how others handle objections like:

"Our budget is frozen for the next year."
"This is really expensive – I don't think we can afford it."

Reply | Forward

Subject: Re:Money objections
Author: Barbara Carnes

Topic: Challenges?
Date: January 3, 2009 6:20 AM

One thing that's worked for me with the frozen budget is:
"Let's look at how the investment can be broken up into some smaller pieces that may be considered expenses rather than capital expenditures."

Has anyone else tried this?

Reply | Forward

Subject: Re:Money objections
Author: Barbara Carnes

Topic: Challenges?
Date: January 3, 2009 6:28 AM

I tried it and it worked pretty well.

Reply | Forward

The best forums are usually on demand. That is, they can be accessed when the trainee wants or needs them. Generate ideas with previous participants or in current training classes. If there is wide variation in types of trainees (see 2 above), consider more than one type of forum.

4. Determine how to be involved in the forum. If the forum is not moderated or reviewed from time to time, trainees may give each other incorrect information, or the focus of the forum could drift to become more of a complaint session. Options for trainer involvement include
   - convening the forum and facilitating discussions
   - checking in and participating on an occasional basis but not taking responsibility for facilitating
   - considering the forum to be "self-service" with no further trainer involvement.

5. Set up the needed technology. It is best to do this in advance of the training if possible to reduce chance of delay when it is time to use the forum.
   - Introduce the forum in the training class to build interest and help trainees see the value.
   - Stay in touch with trainees after the learning event and remind them to use the forum.

Downside

This TIE may not be as effective as it could be if

- Trainees do not have a need or desire to use the skills learned in training. (It may be time to redesign.)
- The forum platform or technology does not fit the participants. For example, a web-based forum may not be the best choice for those who don't have regular or frequent computer or Internet access.
- Most trainees are able to use the new skills correctly and confidently immediately on returning to the job, without need for further support. (Save your energy and use it for something that is needed.)

Variations

- Facilitate an email exchange. Send an email to all participants, posing a specific, open-ended question. Summarize their responses and send back to the group.
- Start an email chain letter. A specific question or problem regarding the training topic is forwarded round-robin to the group.
- Ask a supervisor to facilitate or monitor the forum. (But be sure the supervisor is current with his or her skills.)
- Suggest that participants set up their own forum on an as-needed basis. They may have access to or prefer a particular platform or networking service. However, discuss with them concerns about any confidential or proprietary information being discussed outside the organization's firewall.
- Encourage a vendor to set up a forum for all users of the particular product or process, or use one they may already have in place.

Combine With

Can-Do Attitude, The Proof's in the Pudding, Credit Cards, Trainees as Teachers, Relapse Prevention, Use It or Lose It Checklist, Training Buddies, Sticky Sessions, Webpage

Mind Sweep: Clear Minds of Distractions That Block Learning

Who: trainer/trainee
When: during
Media: face-to-face, e-learning, webinar, teleclass, coaching

It would be nice if participants arrived at the beginning of training with their minds open and receptive. Very few of them actually begin the learning event with the intention of deliberately tuning out the learning material, but too often this is what happens. They show up with their minds full of unfinished projects, issues, discussions, family, children, household projects, emails and voicemails to return, and other things to do. It is a well-established fact that the mind can only hold one idea at a time (although the ideas can move through in rapid succession). Therefore, if the learners are thinking about their jobs or their lives, they are not thinking about their training.

Multitasking in some organizations has become an expectation. However, human psychology and physiology just doesn't support it. The best way to get the most out of any learning process is to focus.

Trainees need to begin their learning with a mind that is ready to accept new ideas, techniques, and skills. To do this, they need to clear their minds of the clutter and "dust" that lurks there. This technique, borrowed from Gestalt psychology, helps trainees begin the learning with a clear mind, which will increase their ability to absorb new information.

1. Begin by introducing the training in the usual way. Just after the introduction, provide a piece of 8" x 11" paper or ask them to pull one out of their materials.

2. Introduce this activity by saying, "What were you thinking about when you arrived at or began this training?" (Pause) "Is there anything you can do about any of these items right now, while you are in training, without leaving the training—physically or mentally?" The answer should be a universal no. Explain that the mind cannot hold more than one idea at a time and for them to learn what they need in this training, they need to clear their minds of other things.

3. Ask them to write down what was on their mind when they arrived or began training: calls to return, quantity of emails in their inbox, projects they're working on, people they need to see, kids, spouses, household issues, and so forth (provide a nice long list of examples). Pause while they write.

4. Have them fold their paper into thirds, like a letter (or provide an envelope), and write on the outside: After Training. Then ask them to take their paper, their phone, laptop, and any other work materials they have brought with them and put them out of view on the floor, on a table at the back of the room, and so on. This is also a good opportunity to remind them to turn phones and pagers off or put them on vibrate.

5. Ask them to close their eyes and imagine a vacuum sweeper: not a powerful one that sucks the breath away, but a gentle vacuum that works quietly. Imagine that this vacuum is sitting right next to their head, gently whirring. Now it's sucking out their distracting thoughts, leaving a clean brain and mind. Ask them to visualize a clean white space, like a white board with nothing on it. This is their mind at the present time. It will be filled with new skills and thoughts throughout the training.

6. Ask them to open their eyes, pause, and begin the training.

7. After breaks, invite participants to add to their lists, and let the vacuum refresh and clear their minds again.

Downside

This TIE may not be as effective as it could be if

- the culture of the organization is such that people become upset when separated—even psychologically—from their work or their phone
- participants are expecting calls or, worse, are expecting to do other work during the learning event
- people experience "separation anxiety" when asked to put away their phones or laptops
- learners resist the vacuum visualization aspect of this activity, considering it too "touchy feely."

Variations

- Omit step 5. The technique isn't as effective this way but doing so may reduce resistance.
- Have participants pause and think about everything that is on their mind, rather than write.
- Instead of a vacuum sweeper metaphor, use a box. Participants visualize putting what is on their mind into the box. (This can be a communal box for the entire group, or their own private box.) This metaphor may work better than the vacuum in an e-learning design.
- Provide an actual box or basket, ask participants to put their names on the papers (on which they have written what is on their mind). Pass the box around or circulate with it, having them put their papers into the box or basket. Return their papers to them at the end of the learning event.

Combine With

Protect Participants

Relapse Prevention: Facilitate a Powerful Discussion With Proven Results

Who: trainer/participant
When: during/after
Media: face-to-face, e-learning, webinar, teleclass, coaching

This TIE started with an activity used by professionals in addiction treatment programs. Toward the conclusion of their treatment, participants were asked to consider and discuss a series of questions to help them anticipate, cope, and deal with any potential lapse or slip back into their prior habitual behaviors. Robert Marx, an early researcher of training transfer, decided to try using these "relapse prevention discussions" to tackle the training transfer problem in corporate training. He reasoned that both addiction treatment and workplace training involve maintaining behavior changes. His research, as well as later studies and anecdotal reports,[1] has confirmed that these structured relapse prevention discussions are effective in helping participants transfer learning to the workplace, just as they are in helping individuals deal with potential relapses of addictive behaviors.

Although not widely used in workplace learning, the relapse prevention technique shows great potential for a relatively quick and easy way to make learning stick.

It is important to follow the steps of the relapse prevention discussion in the order given, without skipping any steps (see figure 3-7):

1. Summarize the key learning points of the training. Emphasize behaviors and skills learned that should be used in their jobs.
2. Ask what the benefits are to you, to your team/department, and to your organization for using these skills.

---

[1] Some of the empirical studies have been limited by small sample size and other issues. Better research studies are needed to complement those that currently exist.

Figure 3-7. Sample Relapse Prevention Questions

Summarize Key Learning Points/Skills
- What are the benefits of using these skills?
- For you?
- Your team?
- Our company?
- What obstacles might get in the way?
- How can you overcome these obstacles?

3. Ask what some possible obstacles are that might keep you from doing this/ these things.
4. Ask what some ways are to overcome these obstacles? Enlist the help of the class to generate options.

That's it. The entire discussion should take 10-15 minutes, maybe a bit longer for a larger or a more talkative class.

For webinars or other real-time virtual learning, use the summary and questions in the same way as in the classroom, or in a follow-up email. For blended learning or asynchronous e-learning, pose the questions in discussion threads, one question per thread. Be sure to respond to comments and facilitate this virtual discussion. For one-on-one or group coaching sessions, use this discussion toward the end of the coaching or as the person being coached is ready to use a skill or behavior.

Downside

This TIE may not be as effective as it could be if

- the trainer's summary does not pinpoint specific behaviors or skills that participants need to use in their jobs
- the training design does not do a good job of helping participants see how the behaviors and skills learned in the training can be applied to their jobs

- there isn't sufficient time at the end of training for the discussion
- the discussion is held after the specified end time for the training. (Trainees usually "shut down" mentally to some extent once the advertised end time is reached.)

Variations

- Ask participants to mention or list their key learning points or "takeaways" as the beginning step in the discussion.
- Have participants summarize the training by writing the three things they are going to do differently and/or the three key skills they want to be sure to remember. Then proceed with the discussion.
- Provide the discussion questions to managers so they can use the discussion when coaching or training their employees. Be sure to share with them the research on the effectiveness of this discussion technique.
- Send a summary of the discussion to participants' managers.
- Capture participant comments on a flip chart. Transcribe (or use a high-tech flip chart that makes copies) and send to each participant approximately three weeks later, with a follow-up note. Put the points in the body of the email, not in an attachment for easy reading.
- Have participants write their responses to the relapse prevention discussion questions. Provide a form for doing this.
- Use the relapse prevention summary and questions in a follow-up email after the learning event. Be sure to ask participants to send their responses back. Consider copying their supervisor on the email with the questions and on their response.

Combine With

Boss Briefing/Debriefing, Can-Do Attitude, Credit Cards, Use It or Lose It Checklist, Sticky Sessions

Use It or Lose It Checklist: Commit Participants to After-Training Action

Who: trainer/trainee
When: during/after
Media: face-to-face, e-learning, webinar, teleclass, coaching

One of the key reasons people fail to transfer learning to their work is the "use it or lose it" factor. When they take a class, participants continue to perform their usual work responsibilities before and after the class. Participants involved with learning and coaching most often face larger-than-usual workloads when they return to their jobs. They dive into their work and before they know it, their newfound learning has begun to fade.

Research has consistently shown that trainees are less likely to transfer their learning to their jobs when they aren't given opportunities to use the new learning in the work setting. Other related studies have found that when normal workloads and duties are adjusted to provide opportunities to perform and practice the new skills, the training is much more likely to stick.

The Use It or Lose It Checklist is a way to capture specific actions and activities the trainees should, want to, and plan to do to put into practice what they have learned. Whether the list is provided to the trainees by the trainer or coach, or whether they develop it themselves, the checklist provides an easy-to-follow means to encourage opportunity to practice and therefore increase the chances that the learning will stick.

1. Review the learning objectives. Identify specific skills and actions the learner should be able to perform—or perform better—after training. Be prepared to suggest these to trainees at the conclusion of the learning event.

2. Near the conclusion of the learning event or module of a multiple session training, ask participants to list those things that they plan to do to put their training to use. Suggest they think about what they can do as soon as they return to work.

3. Ask them to write these things on a Use It or Lose It Checklist form that has five to 10 spaces.

4. Review their checklists and make suggestions for more specific checklist items as necessary (see table 3-2).

5. Provide accountability by asking participants to email a summary of their completed Use It or Lose It Checklist form with the results column completed to their supervisor or to the trainer.

6. Send a reminder email to participants one week afterward if their form hasn't been received (see figures 3-8 and 3-9). Consider copying their supervisor.

Downside

This TIE will not be as effective as it could be if

- the actions, activities, skills, and/or behaviors provided on the list are not relevant to participants' jobs
- the actions, activities, skills, and/or behaviors provided on the list cannot reasonably be practiced within the first week after training (the Success Stories and Lessons Learned TIE may be a better approach in this case)
- the priorities of the participants' supervisor do not fit with the checklist items
- participants are not committed to learning the new skills and behaviors (they took the training for other reasons).

Table 3-2. Examples of Specific Checklist Items

More Specific	Less Specific (and Less Desirable)
Disassemble and reassemble a T31	Put together a chip card assembly
Answer at least five support calls—real or simulated with your manager—each day for the first week	Answer support calls for the new system
Conduct a feedback session using the three steps from this training, with at least three direct reports within the first three days	Meet with your employees and try these techniques
Use a different closing technique from the class in at least five calls during the first week	Use the new techniques

Figure 3-8. Sample Use It or Lose It Letter to Participant*

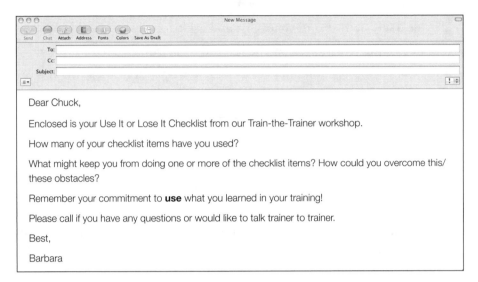

*Note how Relapse Prevention is combined with Use It or Lose It here.

Figure 3-9. Use It or Lose It Checklist

✓ I recognize that I need to use the skills and information I have just learned in training or I will lose it/them. Therefore, I am listing below specifically what I will do **as soon as I return to my job.**

_____

_____

_____

_____

_____

_____

Variations

- Provide participants with a predetermined Use It or Lose It Checklist that contains items that each trainee should do immediately upon returning to their job.
- Ask trainees' supervisor or trainees themselves to review the predetermined list and make additions, corrections, or suggestions so that the link

between the learning objectives and the skills and activities on the job is as tight as possible.

- Provide a few items for the checklist and ask participants to add some.
- Instruct participants to review the list and to personalize it with their notes; for example, adding names of people with whom they will talk or practice.
- Include a column in the form for the trainee's supervisor or peer to sign off.
- Participants receive the Use It or Lose It Checklist prior to training, with instructions to plan their posttraining work schedule accordingly.
- Offer a prize or other reward for completing the list.
- For coaching or ongoing group learning, use a Use It or Lose It Checklist form at the beginning and at the end of each coaching session to provide a framework for discussing successes/challenges since the last meeting and to provide focus for the current meeting.

Combine With

Boss Briefing/Debriefing, Strategy Link, Can-Do Attitude, Credit Cards, Success Stories and Lessons Learned, Training Buddies, Sticky Sessions

Training Buddies: Encourage Peer Learning Support Before, During, and After Training

Who: trainee/trainer
When: before/during/after
Media: face-to-face, e-learning, webinar, teleclass, coaching

A special friend available for support and guidance is a popular way to make new behaviors stick—in weight loss programs, parenting classes, even health self-examination. Apply the sample principle to workplace learning and development: before, during, and/or after the learning event, each trainee has a special buddy to check in with for support, motivation, accountability, reminders, and peer guidance.

A one-on-one relationship with a peer is a good way for buddies to support one another. When they arrive at the class for the first time, particularly if the class is off site, participants may appreciate having a preassigned training buddy to get acquainted with. Trainees who are introverted often appreciate the opportunity to get acquainted with one other person a little more in depth. During the training, buddies spend time together discussing what they are learning. They may both have the same question or an information gap that they can figure out together. Their self-confidence may need a boost before they try the new skill in the class or on the job. After they use a new skill, buddies may want to share their experience—positive and not-so-positive—with someone who understands and who is not their immediate supervisor.

The relationship with a training buddy can also provide accountability to use the new skills on the job or to engage in other follow-up activities. Often if one asks, "What will happen if I don't use a particular new skill?" and the answer is, "Nothing," then there is no motivation to do it. A training buddy provides a measure of motivation because when the question is asked, "What will happen if I don't use a particular new skill?" the answer will be "I'll have to tell my training buddy why I didn't."

A training buddy can also provide helpful reminders beforehand to help his or her partner remember to use skills and to do other related tasks. Calendar ticklers and other desk assistants mean that this reminding takes almost no time at all—a matter of one to two minutes.

Many times throughout the class and at the very end, the instructor reminds participants to ask if they have questions. Some participants do ask questions during the training; others hold back. A very few participants contact the trainer after the learning event is over, although it is reasonable to think that many more have questions and for many reasons do not contact their trainer. Participants are much more likely to ask questions of a fellow classmate because the classmate is usually more available than the trainer, who may have others asking for assistance. The classmate peer is usually more approachable in the eyes of the trainee as well.

1. Assign training buddies or allow them to choose. This may take place before the learning event, during the learning event, or at the very end of the learning event. There are advantages for each time point.
   - If training buddies are assigned or chosen before the learning event, they have at least one person to talk with and get to know. This usually increases the trainees' comfort level, which in turn makes it easier for them to learn.
   - If training buddies are assigned or chosen at the beginning of the learning event, their attendance is guaranteed, they are already there. There is no risk of someone not having their training buddy show up. Pairing training buddies at the beginning of the training provides a good opportunity for them to share their learning goals and why they are in the training class.
   - If training buddies are assigned or chosen at the end of the learning event, they are, it is hoped, already thinking about using their new skills on the job. The timing is right to discuss what type of support they would like to get from their training buddy.
2. Training buddies are more likely to stay in touch with each other afterward if they are in close proximity to one other—in the same department,

plant, or city—or if they have similar job titles. In a classroom, it is usually quicker and easier to provide this guidance and then allow them to choose. In an e-learning or webinar format, usually it is quicker and easier to assign them. If the number of participants is uneven there will be one trio.

3. Allow time(s) throughout the training for the training buddies to discuss key learnings and applications with each other.

4. Provide preprinted or blank cards for buddies to record each others' contact information, best ways to get in touch, learning objectives, possible obstacles, and how they would like to be supported and reminded.

5. Use the training buddies to form small activity/discussion groups: two to three pairs per small group.

6. After the learning event, it is helpful for the trainer to remind buddies to stay in touch with one another. Consider offering a small incentive or prize for the buddies who stay in touch with one another for a specified time period—six weeks or three months, for example.

7. Informing the trainees' managers about the training buddies provides additional motivation to stay in touch (see figure 3-10).

Figure 3-10. Sample Training Buddy Email to Supervisor

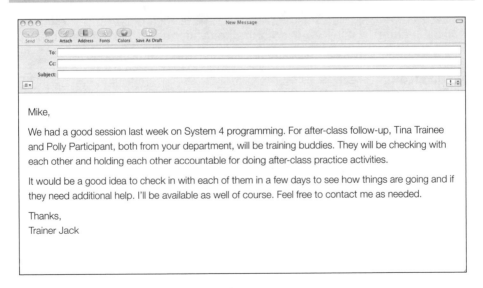

Mike,

We had a good session last week on System 4 programming. For after-class follow-up, Tina Trainee and Polly Participant, both from your department, will be training buddies. They will be checking with each other and holding each other accountable for doing after-class practice activities.

It would be a good idea to check in with each of them in a few days to see how things are going and if they need additional help. I'll be available as well of course. Feel free to contact me as needed.

Thanks,
Trainer Jack

Downside

This TIE may not be as effective as it could be if

- training buddies don't see value or benefit in staying in touch with one another after the learning event
- training buddies do not have much in common with one another—job titles, ways they will use the training
- training buddies have not had much opportunity to interact with one another during training; the more interaction time, the more cohesion is developed
- trainees forget about their training buddy after returning to their job
- trainees master the skills and have no need for support, accountability, reminders, or guidance when they return to work.

Variations

- Provide training buddy assignments to be completed during or after class to give more structure to their time together.
- Assign the trainees' manager to be their training buddy, after the learning event.
- Assign or allow trainees to choose multiple training buddies. Although some accountability may be lost (due to the group dynamic known as social loafing), having more than one training buddy increases the chances that a buddy will be available when needed and will follow through as requested.

Combine With

Can-Do Attitude, Seeds, Apples, Target Objectives, Success Stories and Lessons Learned, Relapse Prevention

Sticky Sessions: Drive Learning Home With After-Training Application Meetings

Who: trainer/trainee
When: after
Media: face-to-face, e-learning, webinar, teleclass

A sticky session is a small group meeting held one to three weeks after the learning event or in between multisession learning events. The purpose of this session is to foster application of the learning (to make it "sticky") by providing an opportunity for facilitator and participants to talk informally about what they learned and how they are using it or plan to use it. Doing this allows them to benefit from one another's experiences and reinforces what they have learned.

The structure should be loose. It is usually best for the workplace learning professional to attend because questions may come up that need responses. If this person is not able to attend, it is helpful to have a designated facilitator who may be another trainer or perhaps a manager—someone who can answer questions and help participants bridge their learning to their jobs.

The small group setting (10-15 people maximum) allows reasonable "air time" for each participant to speak, share experiences, and ask questions. If the learning event itself had more than 15 participants and all of them will participate, schedule multiple sticky sessions, dividing participants according to department/division, geography, or in other logical ways. Sessions could be held concurrently, and the trainer could move back and forth between them. The sessions could also be held virtually. Telephone sessions would work especially well for this. The webinar or e-learning media will probably seem instructor led and may not encourage open dialogue.

Sticky sessions can be considered and scheduled as part of the learning event, requiring everyone to attend, or they can be optional, with only those attending who want to continue discussion and/or have questions. If a sticky session is optional, often the quiet participants attend. Perhaps this is because they are more comfortable talking and asking questions in a smaller group.

A sticky session may be especially useful when participants have attended an outside learning event, such as a public workshop or conference, assuming at least three people from the organization have attended. The sticky session then becomes a way to talk about how to "drive the learning home" to the organization. In this case, a workplace learning professional, human resources person, or line manager facilitates the session.

1. Decide whether to make the sticky session optional or mandatory. The learning content and nature of most participants will probably enter heavily into this decision. Will those who need to come attend if they have a choice? Will all participants have an equal need for a sticky session, or will some participants be adept at the skill immediately after the learning event, whereas others need some additional support?

2. Schedule, announce, and publicize the sticky session along with the learning event so that people will understand that it is a part of the learning and mark their calendars accordingly. Sixty to 90 minutes is a good timeframe for a face-to-face sticky session, 45 to 60 minutes for a virtual session.

3. During the course of the learning event, remind participants of the upcoming sticky session. If time is tight in the learning event itself, save some discussions that would normally occur then for the sticky session.

4. Do not over-prepare for the sticky session. It is helpful to have a handout or two, perhaps one piece of new material not covered in the original training. It is also helpful to have an open-ended question or two that targets how key learning points are being used. Beyond this, be prepared to zip your lip so participants can discuss freely.

5. During the sticky session, provide an introduction of no more than one to two sentences. Then ask one of the open-ended questions previously prepared. Allow the discussion to free-flow, interjecting only if the discussion lags or gets seriously off track.

6. If discussion lags, share the handout or new material previously prepared. Provide two to three minutes of explanation, no more. Then let them discuss.

7. Throughout the session, facilitate, don't train or present. The goal is to allow participants to discuss, share, and perhaps even commiserate.

Downside

This TIE may not be as effective as it could be if

- Participants do not attend. Busy schedules, demanding managers and customers, vacation plans, and so on, may interfere with attendance.
- Managers and supervisors of the participants do not see the value in a sticky session and therefore will not allow or encourage trainees to participate. If this is the case, the sticky session should be sold to managers as part of the learning event.
- The trainer does not have the time to conduct sticky sessions.
- The trainer gets carried away in the sticky session and uses it as another opportunity to teach rather than facilitate.
- The trainer or whoever facilitates the session allows the discussion to drift to other topics rather than focus on the skills learned and how to apply them.

Variations

- Use a different medium for the sticky session than was used for the learning event. This is especially useful if attendees have traveled to attend a face-to-face learning event. A webinar or teleconference can provide similar opportunities for discussion.
- Use an email (discussion threads) discussion group. This can be set up with most email software. Once the discussion group has been set up, post two to three open-ended questions in separate threads. Monitor the discussion daily. Allow three to five days for the discussion, then close

it. Allow the discussion to flow, intervening only if it gets seriously off track.

- Provide a sticky session for people who have attended different conferences or external learning events. Use global, open-ended questions in this case, such as "What was the most significant learning/information that you will use back at work?"
- Include people who did not attend the original learning event or conference but have an interest in the subject.
- Ask a trainee's manager or another member of the learning and development staff to facilitate the session. This may provide new perspective.
- Designate one of the participants to facilitate a sticky session.

Combine With

Boss Briefing/Debriefing, Can-Do Attitude, The Proof's in the Pudding, Seeds, Trainees as Teachers, Success Stories and Lessons Learned, Use It or Lose It Checklist

Screen Saver: Provide Desktop Messaging for Real-Time Reminders

Who: trainer/trainee
When: after
Media: face-to-face, e-learning, webinar, teleclass, coaching

Positive mental attitude gurus and marketing and advertising experts have known for years the tremendous power in repetitive messaging. We need only recall popular phrases and sayings to understand their staying power. What people remember they are more likely to do. Consider some of these sayings:

- The Pepsi Generation
- Have a Coke and a Smile
- How many licks does it take to get to the Tootsie Roll center of a Tootsie Pop?

These advertising phrases have not been used for years but many people still remember them or have heard them.

A participant's desktop computer screen saver provides a perfect opportunity to use repetitive messaging to help participants remember a key point, tip, or cautionary note. When the screen is inactive for a period of time, the single sentence or phrase pops up and appears on the screen in various forms. The size, font, rotation, and general appearance of the sentence can usually be determined as well.

The trainee may only see the message briefly before he or she reactivates the screen to begin working again but he or she will perceive these repetitive, although brief, exposures at the conscious or subconscious level. Research on subliminal suggestion has found that people perceive even the smallest, most subtle suggestions and clues and they are able to consciously or subconsciously recall them later.

1. Identify learning that lends itself to a single sentence reminder. Review the learning objectives to get ideas.

2. Develop a single sentence or phrase that captures what the trainee needs to remember or do. Here are some examples that have been used with screen savers:
   - Criticize the behavior, not the person.
   - Always maintain and enhance self-esteem.
   - Activate the safety latch first.
   - Feedback first.
   - Always complete documentation before closing out.
   - Fast pace, friendly tone.
   - Eye, hi, good-bye.

3. Introduce the phrase or sentence during training as a part of the learning in the materials, the visuals, on posters, reminder cards, on the back of name tents, and so forth. Remember, just because the message has been delivered once doesn't mean it has registered with participants. The goal is repetitive messaging.

4. Toward the conclusion of the class or coaching, provide the sentence or phrase to trainees along with instructions on how to use it in their screen saver (see below). In classroom settings, a note card handout works well. For webinars, send the instructions in a follow-up email. For e-learning, post the instructions as an announcement or include as a pop-up or as a part of the training materials.

> Steps for changing a screen saver vary from system to system. The screen saver is usually changed on a personal computer under the Control Panel, under the Display file or tab, or on a Mac under the Apple menu, System Preferences. Consult your system's help function or Internet browser for specific information on specific operating systems.

5. Send a separate reminder after the learning event that repeats the instructions and reminds participants to install the phrase in their screen saver.

Downside

This TIE may not be as effective as it could be if

- the trainee doesn't know how to install the phrase as their screen saver and doesn't understand the instructions
- company information technology permissions do not allow this type of screen saver
- trainees are using other screen savers they prefer (suggest they use this phrase just for a specified period of time, such as every one to two months, then they can use other screen savers again)
- the phrase or sentence is too complicated to remember easily.

Variations

- Develop and provide several phrases or sentences and ask participants to choose one.
- Develop several phrases or sentences and send these to participants one at a time after training, requesting that they change their screen saver periodically. Be sure to include the instructions each time.
- Provide a sentence or phrase on a hard copy reminder card as an option for those who do not want to use it as a screen saver.
- Send the sentence or phrase daily in an email to each participant. Gradually reduce the frequency and discontinue after two months.
- Use a picture reminder instead of a phrase or sentence. A picture or phrase from the workshop itself can be quite effective. To add interest, ask participants to match a phrase with a picture, then send out the winning matches to be used as screen savers.
- Ask participants to install a picture as their desktop rather than as a screen saver.

Combine With

Can-Do Attitude, Credit Cards, Success Stories and Lessons Learned, Relapse Prevention, Use It or Lose It Checklist, Webpage

Webpage: Keep Learning Alive With Resources and Support

Who: trainer/trainee/trainee's supervisor
When: before/after
Media: face-to-face, e-learning, webinar, teleclass, coaching

Most learning and development departments have websites that usually contain descriptions of courses and other services the department provides, along with a means for class registration. Few if any learning and development department websites contain class-specific material beyond a brief description and outline for those who may want to register for the class.

A webpage specifically for those who have attended a particular class provides an on-demand resource for participants to use when they need it, as they need it. They can use it to be reminded about specifics from the learning event and when they would like to access additional information and other resources. The content-specific webpage also provides one more touch point to help participants understand how and why this training is important for the organization and for their jobs.

Include a variety of resources on the webpage, depending on the nature of the learning content. Ideas include

- pre-work assignments
- articles and website links to additional information
- quizzes or self-assessments that would otherwise be done in class (saves time)
- podcast or short video segment of a senior leader discussing the benefits of the learning
- podcast or short video segment of additional content not included in the learning event
- FAQs
- message board to post tips and experiences, or even jokes
- learning content summary for participants' supervisors.

Templates and other user-friendly web software make it easier than ever to create attractive, functional webpages in a short period of time. The webpage should be conceived and planned by the trainer or instructional designer and could also be developed by this person, or another individual who knows the software.

Regardless of how it is developed, the webpage should be ready and accessible when learners need and want it. If the webpage will be used primarily for additional resources, it should be live and ready immediately at the conclusion of the learning event, if not before. Naturally, if the webpage will be used for prework, it needs to be available before the class.

1. Identify the learning content the webpage will cover. In most cases, this should be the learning content in a single class. If the class and the learning content are extensive, however, it may make sense to focus the webpage on only one area or aspect of the content. Avoid the temptation to include more than one class or content area with a single webpage because this will dilute the focus.

2. Review the learning objectives and determine what participants should be doing, or doing differently, in their jobs as a result of the training. Make a list of all possible things for before and after the learning event that will provide additional information, motivation, tips, guidance, and suggestions for applying the learning. In other words, determine what to cover on the page.

3. Now determine how the material will be covered. See the above list for ideas.

4. Gather and create the necessary materials: scan articles (be mindful of copyrights), create audio and/or video files, develop FAQs, and so on.

5. Connect with necessary technical resources. How is the department website or web area put together? What software was used? Who is available for tech support assistance and to do the programming, if necessary?

6. Determine how this webpage will be accessed. Will there be a link from the home page? Will it be password protected? Will this page silently

reside within the site, accessible to participants and other visitors only by specific URL address?

7. Determine how this webpage will be used. Will participants be directed there before the learning event? After? Both? Will participants' managers be asked to visit the site to become acquainted with the learning content?

8. Armed with ideas, sketch how the webpage will look: overall look and feel, relevant links, and so on. Remember it is not training or e-learning. Think resource.

9. Develop the page. Draft in word processing form or directly in web software. Some trainers prefer to write in word processing software and copy and paste into web software; others prefer to write directly into the web software. Templates and user-friendly software are available for those without programming skills.

10. Publicize the page. Send trainees and perhaps their managers a link to the page before the training. Introduce or remind participants about the site during training. Consider using a screen shot of the page to provide a visual reminder. Send a follow-up email after the learning event with a link to the page. Consider incentives for visiting the page, such as the first five visitors will receive a prize. Most people love getting their company's logo items, and these are often easy to obtain from other departments for prizes.

Downside

This TIE may not be as effective as it could be if

- learners do not have easy intranet or Internet access or do not access the organization's intranet regularly as a part of their jobs
- the appearance of the webpage is unattractive and boring (too much text without graphics and other visual relief makes for an unfriendly webpage that will not be used as well or as often)
- the content of the webpage is not useful: although it may be helpful to include material from the training on the webpage, if it is merely a rehash of what has already been learned, most participants will not find it helpful
- participants forget about the site (send periodic reminders).

Variations

- A webpage "for supervisors only" that provides guidance on how to prepare participants for the learning and how to help them apply it. Include checklists on what to cover with each trainee beforehand and afterward, drafts on what to tell participants about the training, what to watch for as trainees try out new skills and behavior, and "executive summaries" of key content pieces from the training.
- An entire website that contains a training course or training series. Although this takes more time and resources to develop, it may be appropriate for progressive series of classes or learning content that requires a lot of follow-up information.
- Regular update feed that streams content updates to participants as new content becomes available, in addition to or instead of the webpage.
- A few paragraphs on the training department website that detail after-class materials. For example, the home page of the training department website could have a menu item entitled "After-Class Follow-Up." Clicking on this menu item would reveal a page with several paragraphs devoted to each course. These paragraphs could contain links to resources.
- A vendor-developed website or webpage dedicated specifically to support the learning event. If the learning materials are published by an external training company or if a consultant or vendor has provided the learning event, they may have—or consider having—a website devoted to supporting particular learning content.

Combine With

Boss Briefing/Debriefing, Success Stories and Lessons Learned, Use It or Lose It Checklist, Podcasts, Protect Participants, Strategy Link

Chapter 4

Conclusion

Training transfer has come a long way, and it has a long way yet to go. I first began writing about training transfer some 20 years ago. At the time very little information was available on the subject. My co-author Dora Johnson and I developed the first set of TIEs in our book *Making Training Stick,* based on our own experiences as trainers and on conversations with other trainers we knew or had met in the course of our many presentations to ASTD conferences, chapter meetings, and other trainer gatherings.

As the years progressed, more scholarly research was conducted on training transfer. I also began to notice that trainers and coaches shared techniques and strategies with me that they had developed and were using to promote transfer. People were actually starting to use these techniques! Today in trainer groups when I ask, as I often do, "What do you and your organization do to make training stick?" I am very often pleased to hear about specific, documented strategies and techniques that many trainers and coaches are using to increase on-the-job use of skills learned in training.

Although more workplace learning professionals understand the need for and are using training transfer strategies, there is still much that can and should be done to promote stickiness in workplace learning. Using TIEs is an obvious first step. In addition, I propose three additional thoughts.

Clarify What Works

First, we need to get clear about what works in a particular organization and what doesn't. During the past few years it has become clear that transfer strategies and TIEs are not one size fits all. The same strategies and techniques that are successful in promoting training transfer in one organization will fail miserably in another organization. The same strategies and techniques that are successful in promoting transfer for some job roles will not be successful for other job roles. For example, "learning by doing" sorts of TIEs are certainly not appropriate for high-risk job roles, such as pilots and surgeons, but will work well for other job roles. Specific checklists of skills to practice after return to work are not appropriate for senior leaders, but will work well for many other roles. It is important for organizations and training departments to get clear about what works in their culture and with the job roles they work with.

Unify Efforts to Transfer Learning

Second, there should be some degree of unity in transfer efforts within the organization or department. The TIEs in this book can be used and varied according to the tastes of each trainer. They are most effective, however, if they are used consistently within an organization, across many training programs or coaching clients, when appropriate. My research—formal and informal—shows that most often efforts to support transfer within an organization could be more consistent and focused than they are. For example, if all managers in a particular organization know that they will receive a post-training checklist of things they need to cover with someone after training or coaching and if they understand that performing this checklist is viewed by their manager as an important part of their job duties, then the checklist is more likely to get done and to have maximum effect. In this way transfer strategies become woven into the fabric of the organization and become "the way we do things around here."

Establish Feedback Measurements

Last, we need feedback. Training transfer needs to be measured to determine what is being used and what isn't. Although computing ROI and proving the value of training is important work, it is usually complicated, time consuming, and not budgeted. A recent study found that only 2.6 percent of the average training budget is spent on evaluation, and this number has actually decreased in the past 10 years. If we are ever to have specific, usable information about what is sticking and being used and what is not, we need to look at key operational metrics, not only within the organization as a whole but especially for particular departments and job roles. As part of our training and coaching preparation, we need to have conversations with the managers of the people we are training to determine how to best measure what has been learned and what is being applied to the job. Then we need to find practical, time-efficient ways to check back after the learning and obtain measured feedback so that we can celebrate what is working and fix what is not.

A Journey Begins With the First Step

The TIEs in this and in my previous books are just the tip of the iceberg for training transfer. Senior management support and a culture of learning within the organization are sure ways to increase transfer of learning to the job. When this happens, TIEs are helpful additions to the structured learning. In most organizations, however, there are gaps—often quite large—between what people learn in structured programs and what senior management and the culture model and reinforce. In these cases, TIEs are critical to the transfer of learning and to the continuing value of workplace learning.

An old Chinese saying is that a journey of a thousand miles begins with a single step. We have taken many steps in our journey and we have many yet to go, until most trainees and coaching clients in most organizations apply to their jobs what they have learned in training. With every learning event, with each trainee, let us endeavor to advance in the journey, one step at a time, one class, and one learner at a time. By doing so we can help each learner do his or her job more effectively, which in turn helps the organization be more effective. We can make a real difference.

Please visit www.MakeLearningStickResources.com for tips, tools, techniques, and ongoing dialogue on making learning stick.

References and Resources

References

Baldwin, T., and J. Ford. 1988. Transfer of Training: A Review and Directions for Future Research. *Personnel Psychology* 41: 63–105.

Bandura, A. 1997. *Self-Efficacy: The Exercise of Control.* New York: W.H. Freeman.

Birren, F. 1961. *Color Psychology and Color Therapy: A Factual Study on the Influence of Color on Human Life.* New Hyde Park, New York: University Books.

Broad, M., and J. Newstrom. 1992. *Transfer of Training.* Reading, MA: Addison-Wesley.

Burke, L., and H. Hutchins. 2007. Training Transfer: An Integrative Literature Review. *Human Resource Development Review* (September): 263–296.

Hill, R., and R. Barton. 2005. Red Enhances Performance in Contests. *Nature* (May 19): 293.

Knowles, M. 1975. *Self-Directed Learning: A Guide for Learners and Teachers.* New York: Association Press.

Kontoghiorghes, C. 2004. Reconceptualizing the Learning Transfer Conceptual Framework: Empirical Validation of a New Systemic Model. *International Journal of Training and Development* 8 (3): 210–221.

Machin, A., and G. Fogarty. 2003. Perceptions of Training-Related Factors and Personal Variables as Predictors of Transfer Implementation Intentions. *Journal of Business and Psychology* 18 (1): 51–71.

Mager, R. 1997. *Analyzing Performance Problems,* 3rd ed. Atlanta, GA: Center for Effective Performance.

Resources

American Society for Training & Development. 2008. *State of the Industry Report.* Alexandria, VA: ASTD Press.

Broad, M., ed. 1997. *Transferring Learning to the Workplace.* Alexandria, VA: ASTD Press.

Broad, M. 2005. *Beyond Transfer to Training: Engaging Systems to Improve Performance.* San Francisco: Pfeiffer.

Cheng, E., and D. Ho. 2001. A Review of Transfer of Training Studies in the Past Decade. *Personnel Review* 30 (1): 102–118.

Color Vision Testing Online, available at http://colorvisiontesting.com. Retrieved September 24, 2009.

Hutchins, H., and L. Burke. 2007. Identifying Trainers' Knowledge of Training Research Findings—Closing the Gap Between Research and Practice. *International Journal of Training and Development* 11 (4): 236–264.

Kirkpatrick, D., and J. Kirkpatrick. 2005. *Transferring Learning to Behavior.* San Francisco: Berrett-Koehler.

Knowles, M. 1980. *The Modern Practice of Adult Education: From Pedagogy to Andragogy.* Englewood Cliffs, NJ: Cambridge Adult Education.

Saks, A., and M. Belcourt. 2006. An Investigation of Training Activities and Transfer of Training in Organizations. *Human Resource Management* 45 (4): 629–48.

Salas, E., and J. Cannon-Bowers. 2001. The Science of Training: A Decade of Progress. *Annual Review of Psychology* 52: 471–99.

Zenger, J., J. Folkman, and R. Sherwin. 2005. The Promise of Phase 3. *Training and Development* (January): 30–34.

For a more comprehensive list of resources, consult www.MakeTrainingStick.com.

About the
Author

Barbara Carnes has been a trainer for more than 30 years, first as a corporate trainer for Sprint North Supply and later as a trainer and external consultant for Carnes and Associates, the company she founded in 1982. She holds a PhD in human and organizational systems from The Fielding Institute, where she penned her 1993 dissertation, "Training Transfer: An Exploration of the Factors Which Account for Behavior Change Following a Training Program." She is the co-author of the book *Making Training Stick* and its companion *Making Training Stick: A Training Transfer Field Guide.* Carnes is a full professor on the practitioner faculty at Webster University where she teaches human resource development graduate courses, and she also teaches in the doctoral program for The University of Phoenix. She is a past president of the St. Louis Metro chapter of the American Society for Training & Development and also for the Human Resource Management Association, a chapter of the Society of Human Resources Management. Carnes writes a newsletter, *Sticky Notes*, and regularly conducts train-the-trainer workshops and presentations. She can be reached at BCarnes@MakeTrainingStick.com.

Index